The Syntax of FOCUS and WH-Questions in Japanese
A Cross-Linguistic Perspective

The Syntax of FOCUS and WH-Questions in Japanese
A Cross-Linguistic Perspective

Yuko Yanagida

HITUZI SYOBO Publishing

Copyright©Yuko Yanagida 2005
First published 2005

Author : Yuko Yanagida

All rights reserved. Except for the quotation of short passages for the purposes of criticism and review, no part of this publication may be reduced, stored in a retrieval system, or transmitted in any form or by any means, electronic, mechanical, photocopying, recording or otherwise, without the written prior permission of the publisher.
In case of photocopying and electronic copying and retrieval from network personally, permission will be given on receipts of payment and making inquiries. For details please contact us through e-mail. Our e-mail address is given below.

Hituzi Syobo Publishing LTD.
5-21-5 Koishikawa Bunkyo-ku Tokyo, Japan 112-0002

phone +81-3-5684-6871 fax +81-3-5684-6872
e-mail: toiawase@hituzi.co.jp
http://www.hituzi.co.jp/
postal transfer 00120-8-142852

ISBN4-89476-239-0
Printed in Japan

Preface

Japanese is known to be a language in which topics are base-generated in, or moved to, the left peripheral position in sentence structure. There has, however, not been much attention given to focus constituents of Japanese within the generative framework. This book presents extensive discussion on focused constituents in Japanese from both synchronic and diachronic perspectives, and argues that focus plays a crucial role in determining clause structure in Japanese.

The first three chapters of this book are taken from Chapters 1 through 3 of my doctoral dissertation entitled 'Focus Projection and Wh-Head Movement', completed at Cornell University in January 1995. I have retained the same theoretical proposals, empirical arguments, and linguistic data, but I have updated these chapters based on Chomsky's 1995 minimalist framework. Chapters 4 and 5 contain my latest work on focus. In Chapter 4, I present extensive discussion on the focus structure of early Old Japanese. I presented part of this at the Generative Grammar and Classical Japanese Symposium held at Sophia University on July 26, 2003. Chapter 5 is a slightly revised version of my paper entitled "Focus Movement and the Quantificational Structure of Focus Sensitive Operators," which appeared in English Linguistics Vol. 20, in 2003. The English Linguistic Society of Japan has graciously allowed me to reproduce the paper in this book.

I am grateful to my Cornell University adviser John Whitman to whom I owe most of my knowledge in Syntax. I would like to thank Yasuhiko Kato and Tatsusi Motohasi for their many hours of discussion that helped me to prepare for this book. I owe a great deal of my knowledge of Old Japanese to their assistance and valuable comments. I also thank Naoki Fukui, Satoshi Kinsui, Shigeru Miyagawa and Akira Watanabe for comments on my paper presented at the symposium. I am also grateful to the following other people who contributed to my writing this book in one way or another: John Bowers, Gennaro Chierchia, Chris Collins, Jim Gair, Takashi Imai, S.-Y. Kuroda, Fred Landman, Shinsho Miyara, Shin Oshima, Kazuyuki Shigemi and, in particular, Talmy Givón at the University of Oregon, who first taught me linguistics.

I would also express my sincere thanks to Isao Matsumoto and Azusa Matsubara of Hitsuzi Shobo Publishing Co., who spent many hours editing and helping to greatly improve its format. Furthermore, this book was proofread by Mark Feldman and Ken Hinomizu. I am grateful for their prompt work during their own busy times of the year. I express my special thanks to Mark Feldman for his friendship and constant support and encouragement of my work.

Finally, this work was supported by a Grant-in-Aid for Publication of Scientific Research Results from Japan Society for the Promotion of Science (JSPS).

This book is dedicated to my mother, Yomiko Yanagida, who dedicated all her life to her children.

Contents

Preface i

1 Introduction 1
   1.1 Introduction 1
   1.2 Focus Projection and *Wh*-Questions 3
   1.3 Locality Effects 11

2 Focus Projection 13
   2.1 Introduction 13
   2.2 The Focus Projection Hypothesis 14
      2.2.1 Two Types of Focus 14
      2.2.2 The Case of Hungarian 15
      2.2.3 The Case of Chadic Languages (Tuller 1992) 18
      2.2.4 The Case of Japanese 22
         2.2.4.1 Parallelism Between Noun Phrases and Verb Phrases 22
         2.2.4.2 Distribution of VP Adverbs 30
   2.3 Indefinites 35
      2.3.1 Diesing's (1992) Analysis 35
      2.3.2 Interaction between Indefinites and *Wh*-Words 40
   2.4 The Focus Marker *Ittai* 45

3 Clitic Q-Movement 49
   3.1 Introduction 49
   3.2 Head Movement 51
      3.2.1 V-to-I Movement 51
      3.2.2 I-to-C Movement 52

    3.2.3 Verb Second ⋯⋯⋯⋯⋯⋯⋯⋯⋯⋯⋯⋯⋯⋯⋯⋯⋯⋯⋯⋯⋯⋯⋯⋯ 56
3.3 The Clitic Q-Movement Hypothesis ⋯⋯⋯⋯⋯⋯⋯⋯⋯⋯⋯⋯⋯ 60
    3.3.1 Two Types of Head Movement ⋯⋯⋯⋯⋯⋯⋯⋯⋯⋯⋯⋯⋯ 60
    3.3.2 Clitic Movement ⋯⋯⋯⋯⋯⋯⋯⋯⋯⋯⋯⋯⋯⋯⋯⋯⋯⋯⋯⋯⋯ 62
    3.3.3 I-to-C Movement in English ⋯⋯⋯⋯⋯⋯⋯⋯⋯⋯⋯⋯⋯⋯⋯ 66
    3.3.4 Subject-Object Asymmetry ⋯⋯⋯⋯⋯⋯⋯⋯⋯⋯⋯⋯⋯⋯⋯ 68
    3.3.5 *That*-Trace Effects ⋯⋯⋯⋯⋯⋯⋯⋯⋯⋯⋯⋯⋯⋯⋯⋯⋯⋯⋯ 72
3.4 Clitic Q-Movement in Japanese ⋯⋯⋯⋯⋯⋯⋯⋯⋯⋯⋯⋯⋯⋯⋯⋯ 74
    3.4.1 Two Types of Verbals ⋯⋯⋯⋯⋯⋯⋯⋯⋯⋯⋯⋯⋯⋯⋯⋯⋯⋯ 74
    3.4.2 The Q-particle *Ka* ⋯⋯⋯⋯⋯⋯⋯⋯⋯⋯⋯⋯⋯⋯⋯⋯⋯⋯⋯ 75
    3.4.3 Embedded *Wh*-Questions ⋯⋯⋯⋯⋯⋯⋯⋯⋯⋯⋯⋯⋯⋯⋯⋯ 78
        3.4.3.1 Focus Particles and Question Particles ⋯⋯⋯⋯⋯⋯ 79
        3.4.3.2 The Copula *Da* and *Desu* in Japanese ⋯⋯⋯⋯⋯⋯ 80
    3.4.4 Cross-Linguistic Evidence ⋯⋯⋯⋯⋯⋯⋯⋯⋯⋯⋯⋯⋯⋯⋯⋯ 84
3.5 Summary ⋯⋯⋯⋯⋯⋯⋯⋯⋯⋯⋯⋯⋯⋯⋯⋯⋯⋯⋯⋯⋯⋯⋯⋯⋯⋯⋯ 88

4 Case/Focus Particles and Clause Structure Change: Evidence From Early Old Japanese ⋯⋯⋯⋯⋯⋯⋯⋯⋯ 87

4.1 Introduction ⋯⋯⋯⋯⋯⋯⋯⋯⋯⋯⋯⋯⋯⋯⋯⋯⋯⋯⋯⋯⋯⋯⋯⋯⋯ 87
4.2 Reanalysis ⋯⋯⋯⋯⋯⋯⋯⋯⋯⋯⋯⋯⋯⋯⋯⋯⋯⋯⋯⋯⋯⋯⋯⋯⋯⋯ 88
    4.2.1 To-Infinitives ⋯⋯⋯⋯⋯⋯⋯⋯⋯⋯⋯⋯⋯⋯⋯⋯⋯⋯⋯⋯⋯⋯ 88
    4.2.2 *Ga*-Marked Clauses ⋯⋯⋯⋯⋯⋯⋯⋯⋯⋯⋯⋯⋯⋯⋯⋯⋯⋯ 94
4.3 The Position of Subjects ⋯⋯⋯⋯⋯⋯⋯⋯⋯⋯⋯⋯⋯⋯⋯⋯⋯⋯⋯ 97
4.4 Word Order in Early Old Japanese ⋯⋯⋯⋯⋯⋯⋯⋯⋯⋯⋯⋯⋯⋯ 106
    4.4.1 The Basic Word Order Pattern ⋯⋯⋯⋯⋯⋯⋯⋯⋯⋯⋯⋯⋯ 106
    4.4.2 Obligatory Movement of *Wo*-Marked Objects ⋯⋯⋯⋯⋯ 112
4.5 Topicalization of *No*-Marked Phrases ⋯⋯⋯⋯⋯⋯⋯⋯⋯⋯⋯⋯ 116
4.6 Head Initial Hypothesis for Functional Categories ⋯⋯⋯⋯⋯⋯ 121
    4.6.1 Clitic Pronouns in Old Japanese ⋯⋯⋯⋯⋯⋯⋯⋯⋯⋯⋯⋯ 121
    4.6.2 Functional vs. Lexical Categories ⋯⋯⋯⋯⋯⋯⋯⋯⋯⋯⋯ 124
4.7 Focus Projection and Clitic Q-Movement Revisited ⋯⋯⋯⋯⋯⋯ 127
    4.7.1 Clause Initial *Ka* vs. Clause Final *Ka* ⋯⋯⋯⋯⋯⋯⋯⋯⋯ 128
    4.7.2 *No*-Interrogatives vs. *Ka*-Interrogatives ⋯⋯⋯⋯⋯⋯⋯⋯ 133
4.8 Summary ⋯⋯⋯⋯⋯⋯⋯⋯⋯⋯⋯⋯⋯⋯⋯⋯⋯⋯⋯⋯⋯⋯⋯⋯⋯⋯ 137

5 Focus Movement and Semantic Interpretation 139
- 5.1. Introduction 139
- 5.2 Semantic Background 140
- 5.3 Focal Presupposition to Entailment 143
- 5.4 Adverbs of Quantification 145
  - 5.4.1 Association with Focus 145
  - 5.4.2 Quantificational Variability 146
- 5.5 Analysis 149
  - 5.5.1 Proportion Problems 150
  - 5.5.2 Problems with Herburger's Analysis 151
- 5.6 Syntactic Account 153
  - 5.6.1 Diesing's Mapping Hypothesis 155
  - 5.6.2 A Phase-Based Minimalist Approach 155
  - 5.6.3 Covert Focus Movement 157
  - 5.6.4 Two Kinds of Determiners 160
  - 5.6.5 Intervention Effects 162
- 5.7 Concluding Remarks 166

Old Japanese Texts, References 169

To my mother, Yomiko Yanagida

1

Introduction

1.1 Introduction

It has been observed that languages are divided into "subject prominent" and "topic prominent" languages; in the former, the grammatical subject plays a key role in sentence articulation, while in the latter a discourse-pragmatic notion of a topic serves as an essential constituent of sentence structure (cf. Li and Thompson 1976). Within the generative framework, Kiss (1995) has shown that sentence structure in discourse configurational languages is derived by externalizing the topic and/or focus from inside a VP. Although in most discourse configurational languages, both topic and focus constituents move to a particular position in sentence structure, some languages display only one of the two properties. Japanese is notably a topic prominent language. A topic is morphologically marked and there is a left peripheral topic position. A morphologically marked focus, on the other hand, is generally assumed to stay *in-situ*. In this book, I present extensive discussions on focus constructions in Japanese from both synchronic and diachronic perspectives, and argue that focus plays a crucial role in sentence articulation in Japanese syntax.

Chapters 2 and 3 of this book are taken from my 1995 Cornell dissertation titled 'Focus Projection and *Wh*-Head Movement'. Although the basic theoretical proposals and empirical arguments have remained unchanged, these chapters have been updated based on Chomsky's (1995) minimalist framework. In Chapter 2, I discuss cross-linguistic evidence for the existence of a clause internal focus position, which I label Focus Projection (FocP). I present many pieces of evidence that morphologically marked focus phrases in Japanese appear in Spec(FocP), and that this position creates an island for both overt and covert *wh*-movement. In Chapter 3, I argue that the question particle *ka* in Japanese is a clitic that originates in Foc and moves to Comp, which I label clitic Q-movement. While a clitic Q is morphologically realized as *ka* in Japanese, languages that do not possess overt Q have a null clitic Q. I discuss various kinds of head movement across languages, proposing that they are reducible to clitic Q-movement.

Chapter 4 focuses on the discussion of the clause structure of early Old Japanese (OJ). Under a recent minimalist approach to diachronic syntax, it has been proposed that structural change of a clause is viewed as gain or loss of movement caused by a change of abstract features associated with its head (cf. Roberts 1997, Whitman 2000, Roberts and Roussou 2003). A number of empirical observations indicate that the case particle *ga* and *kakari*-focus particles underwent so-called "reanalysis," and that reanalysis of these particles plays a key role in clause structure change in Japanese. Assuming that reanalysis is defined as a change of morphological features associated with a head, I explore the possibility that Japanese clauses are headed by these particles that select a VP on its right. In this way, clause structure change in Japanese can be accounted for by a general principle of syntactic change, recently proposed within Chomsky's (1995) minimalist framework. This chapter is devoted to showing that clause structure change is described as gain or loss of movement, which is caused by morphological change of particles.

Finally, in Chapter 5, I turn to a new facet of the discussion, arguing for a direct link between syntactic and semantic representations of focus. Based on a critical review of Herburger's (2000) semantic theory of focus, I present a number of pieces of evidence that focus *in-situ* in English must undergo covert movement. I argue that covert focus movement employs two structural positions: Spec(FocP) and Spec(CP).

The following sections are taken from Chapter 1 of my 1995 dissertation.

1.2 Focus Projection and *Wh*-Questions

Following the tradition dating back to Baker (1969) of pursuing typological universals concerning *wh*-questions, it has been claimed that languages in which *wh*-words appear to stay *in-situ* involve *wh*-movement as well (cf. Nishigauchi 1986, Watanabe 1992a, b, Aoun and Li 1993). In Chapters 2 and 3, I present a number of arguments for the existence of a clause internal operator projection, which I label Focus Projection (FocP). I claim that FocP has the features [±Q] and [±WH] and it is a landing site for both focus movement and *wh*-movement.[1] Under Chomsky's (1995) minimalist framework, language variation is in part determined by feature strength:

(1) If F is strong, then F is a feature of a nonsubstantive category and F is checked by a categorial feature.   (Chomsky 1995:232)

What follows from (1) is that overt movement is driven by [+strong] features. In English, *wh*-movement of non-subjects exhibits Subject-Auxiliary inversion (SAI) in which the inflected auxiliary is preposed and the subject is postposed. Since Chomsky (1986b), SAI is expressed as a structure-preserving movement of Infl to Comp. While languages like English exhibit I-to-C movement, other Germanic languages exhibit Verb Second, in which the finite verb moves to Comp. Rizzi (1991) suggests that SAI is a special case of Verb Second, called "residual V2." A question arises as to why Infl must move to Comp at all. I propose that a Q-feature is base-generated in Foc, and that this feature is universally strong regardless of whether the language possesses overt *wh*-movement. The Q-feature is forced to move to Comp, as schematically

---

[1] The existence of a clause internal operator position has been suggested in the literature (cf. Laka 1990, Ouhalla 1990, Diesing 1992, Aoun and Li 1993, etc.).

represented as in (2).

(2)
```
            CP
           /  \
         Spec  C'
              /  \
             C    IP
         [Qᵢ+I+C] / \
                Spec I'
                 |  / \
                 t Foc P
                  / \
                Spec Foc'
                    / \
                [tᵢ+Foc] VP
```

I-to-C movement is driven by a strong Q-feature in Foc, which can be either overt or covert depending on the language. I present a number of arguments that Q behaves like a clitic, which is characterized as having the properties of clitic movement.

Note that in some languages, no I-to-C movement takes place in root clauses. Languages which exhibit no I-to-C movement generally allow an overt complementizer in the matrix Comp.[2] For example, *wh*-questions in Kinande, a Bantu language spoken in Zaire, have a complementizer in the matrix Comp. (3) is cited from Rizzi (1990a).

(3) IyondI y⁰ kambale alangIra?
     who that Kambale saw
     'Who did Kambale see?'   (Rizzi 1990a:55)

In *wh*-questions in Egyptian Arabic, an overt complementizer is present in nominal *wh*-questions, as in (4a), while it is absent in non-nominal *wh*-questions, as in (4b).

---

[2] I assume that examples like (3) and (4a) are reduced *wh*-clefts which contain the phonologically unrealized copula.

(4) a. Miin illi [Mona darabit-uh]?
    who that Mona hit-him
    'Who did Mona hit?'
  b. ma'a miin$_i$ Ali xarag e$_i$
    with whom Ali left?
    'With whom did Ali leave?' (Wahba 1984:20)

In languages like French, I-to-C movement is optional in root clauses, as illustrated in (5).

(5) a. Qui elle a rencontré t ?
    'Who she has met?'
  b. Qui a-t-elle t recontré t ?
    'Who has she met?' (Rizzi 1991)

Rizzi and Roberts (1989) indicate that in the Québec dialect of French, the matrix Comp can be occupied by an overt complementizer:

(6) Qui que tu as vu?
   Who that you have seen
   'Who have you seen?' (Rizzi and Roberts 1989:4)

The well-formedness of (6) may account for why French has an option between (5a) and (5b). Whatever principle rules out I-to-C movement in these languages, the lack of I-to-C movement is attributed to the presence of an overt complementizer. Under the clitic Q-movement hypothesis, the Q-feature is base-generated in either clause-internal Foc or Comp. When Q is base-generated in Comp, no head movement is invoked. When it appears in Foc, it raises to a Comp and I-to-C movement results.

In Japanese, *wh*-phrases stay *in-situ* and *wh*-questions are marked by sentence final particles. There are two kinds of particles used in questions, as shown in (7a, b).

(7) a. John-wa nani-o kai-masita-ka?
John-Top what-Acc bought-Q
'What did John buy?'
b. John-wa nani-o katta-no?
John-Top what-Acc bought-Q

In (7a), the *wh*-question is marked by the particle *ka*, while in (7b) it is marked by the particle *no*. From typological considerations, I will argue in Chapters 2 and 3 that *ka*-interrogatives as in (7a) have the same properties as *wh*-questions with syntactic movement in the following points:

(8) a. Foc(us) Projection is instantiated in a position immediately above a VP.
b. The Q-particle *ka* is a morphological realization of Q-features, base-generated in Foc.
c. Q moves to Comp (i.e., clitic Q-movement).

I will show that while *ka*-interrogatives involve I-to-C movement in root clauses, *no*-interrogatives are treated on a par with (3) and (4a) in that there is no I-to-C movement.

In Old Japanese (OJ), the particle *ka* directly marks *wh*-words and a predicate takes the attributive form as opposed to the conclusive form.[3] It is well known that this dependency relation is called "*Kakari-musubi*," as illustrated in (9a, b).

(9) a. Tatuta yama itu-ka koe-namu (M. 83)
Tatsuta Mt. when-Q cross-Aux.At
'When will I cross Tatuta Mountain?'

---

[3] In this book, OJ data are taken from *Manyoshu*, an anthology of Japanese verse completed early in the ninth century. *Manyoshu* is the earliest written record of OJ comprising 4516 long and short poems.

b. Sima-no mifasi-ni dare-ka sumafa-mu (M. 187)
Shima-Gen stair-Loc who-Q live-Aux.At
'Who will live by the stairs fair of the Palace of Shima?'

In OJ, non-interrogative focus phrases are marked by a *kakari*-particle and form *Kakari-musubi*, as in (10a, b).

(10) a. Yosino-no miya-fa ...kumo-so tanabiku (M. 1005)
Yoshino-Gen Villa-Top clouds-Foc trail-At.
'In the Villa of Yoshino, the layers of clouds trail.'
b. Futagi-no miya-fa seno oto-so kiyoki (M. 1050)
Futagi-Gen palace-Top river-Gen sound-Foc clear.At
'In the Palace of Futagi, the sound of the river is clear.'

Note that Sinhala behaves exactly like OJ in that the Q-particle *də* directly marks *wh*-words, and that an *E*-ending appears on the predicate, as opposed to the *A*-ending normally affixed to finite main verbs. Non-interrogative focus elements have the same dependency relations. The following examples are taken from Sumangala (1992).

(11) a. Siri waduwædə keruwA
Siri woodworking do-Past-A
'Siri did woodworking.'
b. Siri mokak-də keruwE
Siri what-Q did-E
'What did Siri do?
c. Citra-i potə kiewuwE
Chitra-Foc book read-E

Kishimoto (1991) indicates that the Q-particle *də* must be adjacent to *wh*-phrases in matrix clauses, while clause final *də* is possible in yes-no questions (see also Sumangala 1992).[4] Thus, consider the following contrast:

(12) a. *Kauru potə gatta-də?
who book bought-Q
'Who bought a book?'
b. oyaa pot-ak gatta-də?
you book-Indef bought-Q
'Did you buy a book?'

Similarly, although I find no example in *Manyoshu* in which *wh*-questions in matrix clauses end with clause final *ka*, there are many instances in which clause final *ka* occurs in yes-no questions, as shown in (13) (cf. Koji 1988).[5]

(13) wa-ga furu tsode-wo imo mitu-ramu-ka (132)
I-Subj wave sleeve-Obj dear see-Aux-Q
'Would my dear have seen the sleeve I waved?'

The above observations indicate that in both Sinhala and OJ, *wh*-phrases are obligatorily focused, and thus marked by a Q-particle. Kishimoto (1991) further shows that in Sinhala, the adjunct *wh*-word *æi* 'why' can not appear with a Q-particle, as illustrated in (14a, b).

---

[4] Sinhala allows *wh*-words in embedded clauses to appear without a Q-particle attached to them, as shown in (i) (cf. Sumangala 1992).
  (i) Chitra [kauru potə gatta-də kiyəla] dannəwa.
     Chitra who book bought-Q that know
     'Chitra knows who bought the book.'
In (i) the *wh*-word is morphologically unmarked, and the Q-particle appears in the clause final position.

[5] There are, however, some examples in which a *wh*-word does not appear with a Q-particle *ka*, as shown below.
  (i) a. isi-wo dare mi-ki (M. 869)
       stone-Obj who see-Past
       'Who saw the stone?'
    b. na-fa ikani omou-ya (M. 3309)
       you-Top how think-FP
       'How do you think (of me)?'

(14) a. Chitra æi paatiya-tə naawe?
Chitra why party-Dat not came
'Why didn't Chitra show up at the party?'
b. *Chitra æi-də paatiya-tə naawe?

In Chapter 2, I argue that the adjunct *wh*-word *why* is treated exactly like morphologically marked *wh*-phrases in that it is a quantifier and appears directly in Spec(FocP).[6] *Wh*-phrases in argument position, on the other hand, are treated as non-quantificational variables and quantificational force comes from a Q-morpheme, which may be adjacent to *wh*-phrases or appear in Comp.

Wahba (1984) indicates that Egptian Arabic possesses two kinds of *wh*-questions, one indicated in (4a) which employs an overt complementizer and the other typed by an overt expletive, as illustrated below:

(Egyptian Arabic)
(15) Huwwa Ali raah feen?
      Q   Ali went where
      'Where did Ali go?'   (Wahba 1984:125)

The expletive *huwwa* in (15) appears only in the initial position, namely the matrix Spec (CP), and is linked to the *wh*-word *in-situ*. McDaniel (1989) shows that German and Romani have two types of *wh*-questions: *wh*-questions with full *wh*-movement and those with partial *wh*-movement. In the latter, it is assumed that a *wh*-phrase moves partially to the lower Spec(CP) and is linked with a Q-expletive generated in the matrix Spec(CP). The German example is given below.

(16) Was glaubt [$_{IP}$ Hans [$_{CP}$ mit wem$_i$ [$_{IP}$ Jakob jetzt t$_i$ spricht]]]
      'WHAT does Hans believe with whom Jakob is now talking?'
                                                   (McDaniel 1989:569)

---
[6] Given that (8a-c) are the properties of *ka*-interrogatives, a detailed analysis of interrogative clauses in Old Japanese will be presented in Chapter 4.

The expletive *kyaa* in Hindi seems to appear in a clause-internal position:

(17) Tum kyaa jaante ho [ki usne kyaa kiyaa]?
      you what know that he what did
      'What do you know that he did?'   (Srivastav 1989:445)

Srivastav (1989) claims that the first *wh*-element *kyaa* is an expletive which appears only in the matrix clause and serves to get a direct question reading of *wh-in-situ*. She claims that this expletive appears in a clause internal position and moves to Spec(CP) at LF.

Assuming that *wh*-questions are typed at S-structure (cf. Cheng 1991), the following diagram indicates whether the given languages possess a Q-particle or a Q-expletive:

(18)

Language	Q-particles	Q-expletives
Japanese	ka	-
Korean	ni	-
Chinese	ne	-
Sinhala	də	-
Kinande	y^0	
German	-	was
Hindi	-	kyaa
Egyptian Arabic	-	huwwa

(18) indicates that *wh*-questions which are typed by an overt Q-particle employ no overt Q-expletive, while those which are typed by a Q-expletive employ no overt Q-particle. These scope markers then serve as a question operator that is linked with a *wh*-phrase.

1.3 Locality Effects

It is known that *wh-in-situ* languages with an overt Q-particle exhibit locality effects; this has led some researchers to claim that *wh*-words *in situ* undergo LF movement (cf. Nishigauchi 1986). Japanese, for example, exhibits *wh*-island conditions.

(19) *John-wa [dare-ga nani-o katta-ka] sitteiru-no?
 John-Top who-Nom what-Acc bought Q know-Q
 *'What did John know who bought t ?'
 *'Who did John know what t bought ?'

When (19) is uttered out of the blue, the *wh*-words inside the *wh*-island cannot take different scope and the sentence is acceptable only as a yes-no question. Similarly, Kim (1989) has reported that Korean does not allow a wide scope reading of *wh*-words inside *wh*-islands:

(Korean)
(20) John-un [nwu-ka mwues-ul sat nunci] mwulet-ni?
 John-Top who-Nom what-Acc bought Q asked-Q
 'Did John ask who bought what?'
 *'What did John ask who bought t?'
 *'Who did John ask bought what?'

Q-expletive languages exhibit the same kind of locality effects holding between the expletive operator and *wh-in-situ*. Consider the following sentences in Egyptian Arabic:

(21) *Huwwa$_i$ Ali nisi [eeh illi [Mona iddat-uh li-miin$_i$]]?
 Q Ali forgot what that Mona gave-it to whom
 'To whom did Ali forget what Mona gave?' (Wahba 1984:152)

Wahba (1984) has reported that in (21), the *wh-in-situ* may not have a matrix scope, showing that Egyptian Arabic induces *wh*-island constraints. *Wh*-island effects are present in German and Romani, as well. The examples below are cited from McDaniel (1989):

(Romani)
(22) *So$_i$ [$_{IP}$ na jane [$_{CP}$ sosqe$_j$ [$_{IP}$ o Demìri mislinol t$_j$ [$_{CP}$ kas$_i$ [$_{IP}$ marjum t$_i$]]]]]?
'WHAT don't you know why Demir thinks whom I hit?'
(McDaniel 1989:577)

(German)
(23) *Was$_i$ fragt [$_{IP}$ sie sich [$_{CP}$ warum$_j$ [$_{IP}$ Hans t$_j$ glaubt [$_{CP}$ wen$_i$ [$_{IP}$ Jakob t$_i$ gelobt hat]]]]]?
'WHAT does she wonder why Hans thinks whom Jakob praised?'
(McDaniel 1989:576)

So in Romani and *was* in German are expletive operators generated in Spec (CP), under McDaniel's analysis. Note that in (22) and (23) the most deeply embedded *wh*-words, *kas* in Romani and *wen* in German, move only partially to the lowest CP. These elements do not cross the intermediate CP, containing *sosqe* or *warum* 'why', yet the sentences induce *wh*-island effects. Following the view that expletive elements must be replaced at LF (cf. Chomsky 1986b), (22) and (23) show strong evidence for the view that the *wh*-word moves covertly to Spec (CP) to replace the *wh*-expletive.[7] The ill-formed sentences, then, may result from this covert movement of *wh*-words. Under the minimalist approach developed by Chomsky (1995), *wh*-island effects are reduced to the Minimal Link Condition (MLC), which is assumed to be a condition on derivations. This book presents a number of pieces of evidence showing that covert movement is subject to this condition as well.

---

[7] Chomsky (1986b) indicates that an expletive element that has no semantic content must be replaced by an overt element at LF due to the Principle of Full Interpretation.

2

Focus Projection

2.1 Introduction

In this chapter, I argue that there is a clause-internal operator projection which I label Foc(us) Projection, and that in languages with syntactic *wh*-movement, *wh*-words move to this position. The existence of an internal operator position has been suggested in the literature. Aoun and Li (1993) propose that in Chinese, there is a Qu projection inside the clause, which determines the sentence type, whether question, indicative, suggestion, etc. (cf. Choe 1982 for Korean). Given the restricted quantifier approach advocated by Lewis (1975) and Heim (1982), Diesing (1992) claims that a quantificational indefinite moves either overtly or covertly to an internal operator position base-generated in the position immediately above a VP. Although non-interrogative focus constituents in languages like English involve no visible focus movement, in languages like Hungarian, focus constituents move obligatorily to a clause internal focus position (cf. Horvath 1986). It is widely acknowledged that Japanese belongs to the group of languages in which there is a left peripheral topic position, but no particular structural position for a focus phrase. In this chapter I argue that phrases marked by a quantificational focus particle appear in Spec(FocP). Following the checking mechanism outlined by Chomsky (1993, 1995), I assume that focused constituents in Japanese possess strong

[+Foc] features which must be checked off in the overt syntax.

2.2 The Focus Projection Hypothesis

2.2.1 Two Types of Focus

Before beginning the discussion which follows, I will be assuming that there are two types of focus; namely, focus which is associated with a non-quantificational variable interpreted as proposed by Heim (1982), and another type of focus which is treated like a true operator and must undergo syntactic movement. To illustrate the difference, let us consider the following examples.

(1) a. John-ga gakusei da.
    John-Nom student be
    'John is a student.'
  b. Tegami-ga kita.
    letter-Nom came
    'A letter came.'

Subject NPs marked with *ga* receive one of two possible readings. The subject in (1a) is interpreted as receiving an "exhaustive listing" reading, while the subject in (1b) receives a "neutral description" (ND) reading (cf. Kuno 1973). Subject NPs marked with *wa* also have two different interpretations.

(2) a. Kujira-wa titekida.
    whale-Top intelligent
    'A whale is intelligent.'
  b. Kujira-wa mieru.
    whale-Top seen
    'A whale can be seen.'

(2a) receives a thematic topic reading, while the subject in (2b) is given a contrastive emphasis. It has been indicated (cf. Diesing 1988) that exhaustive *ga* and contrastive *wa* give a narrow focus reading, in that the constituent marked for focus may not project its focus; i.e., only that constituent itself receives the focus interpretation. The ND reading, on the other hand, gives a wide focus reading in which a constituent marked with focus may project its focus to the entire sentence.

In viewing the interpretation of focus in this way, it seems that there are two types of focus, namely projected focus and unprojected focus. In this chapter, it will be argued that unprojected narrow focus constituents have quantificational force of their own and undergo focus movement. Projected ND focus constituents, on the other hand, are treated as non-quantificational variables and stay *in-situ* in both the syntax and at LF.[1]

In the following, I will examine languages in which unprojected focus constituents move to a position immediately adjacent to the verb. Languages with a unique focus position seem to be basically divisible into two types: languages in which the focus position is immediately before the verb, and languages in which it is immediately after the verb.

2.2.2 The Case of Hungarian

Horvath (1986) shows at length that the canonical word order in Hungarian is SVO, as given in (3).

(3) János megcáfolta a professzor érveit.
     John refuted the professor argument.
     'John refuted the professor's arguments.'   (Horvath 1986:20)

Despite the fact that Hungarian has SVO order, some verbs must be strictly subcategorized to take a PP complement phrase in preverbal position, as

---
[1] While phrases marked by a focus particle appear in Spec(FocP) in Japanese, Japanese differs from Hungarian in that phonologically marked focus phrases can stay *in-situ*, and still allow an exhaustive listing reading. I provide a number of arguments in Chapter 4 and 5 that focus *in-situ* with an exhaustive listing reading involves covert focus movement to the domain of CP.

illustrated in (4) and (5).

(4) a. Mari az asztalra tette az edényeket.
 Mary the table-onto put the dishes
 'Mary put the dishes on the table.'
 b.*Mari tette az asztalra az edényeket.
 Mary put the table-onto the dishes

(5) a. A boszorkány egy csúf békává változtatta a királyfit.
 the witch an ugly frog changed the prince.
 'The witch changed the prince into an ugly frog.'
 b.*A boszorkány változtatta egy csúf békává a királyfit.
 the witch changed an ugly frog the prince.

(Horvath 1986:54)

Verbs such as *put* and *change* in the above examples select two complements: an NP and a PP. In Hungarian, a PP complement must appear in preverbal position. What is peculiar about Hungarian is that this preverbal complement must be postposed in *wh*-questions.

(6) a. Mary mit$_i$ tett az asztalra t$_i$?
 Mary what put the table-onto t$_i$
 'What did Mary put on the table?'
 b.*Mary mit$_i$ az asztalra tett t$_i$?
 Mary what the table-onto put t$_i$ (Horvath 1986:52)

(7) a. A boszorkány kit$_i$ változtatott egy csúf békává t$_i$?
 the witch who changed an ugly frog
 'Whom did the witch change into an ugly frog?'
 b.*A boszorkány kit$_i$ egy csúf békává változtatott t$_i$?
 the witch who an ugly frog changed (Horvath 1986:53)

In (6) and (7), the *wh*-phrase moves to the preverbal position and the complement must appear in the post-verbal position. The complementary distribution between base-generated preverbal complements and *wh*-words leads to the claim that the preverbal position is the landing site of *wh*-words in Hungarian. Horvath further shows that non-interrogative focus phrases must appear in this preverbal position, in which case a preverbal complement is postposed:

(8) a. Attila félt a földrengéstöl.
     Attila feared the earthquake-from
     'Attila was afraid of the earthquake.'
   b. Attila a földrengéstöl félt.
     Attila the earthquake-from feared
     'It was the earthquake that Attila was afraid of.'

(9) a. Mari az asztalra tett az edényeket.
     Mary the table-onto put the dishes.
     'Mary put the dishes on the table.'
   b. Mari az edényeket$_i$ tette az asztatra t$_i$.
     Mary the dishes put the table-onto
     'It is the dishes that Mary put on the table.'

(Horvath 1986:91)

In (8a), the complement phrase appears in the post-verbal position of this 'neutral' sentence, but when the complement phrase appears in an immediately preverbal position as in (8b), it is obligatorily interpreted as the focus of the sentence. Similarly, (9a) is a neutral sentence. In (9b) the complement is focused and must move to the preverbal position. Horvath argues that the feature [+Foc] in Hungarian is assigned by V^0 and that this focus assignment process requires a Spec-Head relation between the element in the preverbal position and the verb.

2.2.3 The Case of Chadic Languages (Tuller 1992)

Tuller (1992) has described two types of Chadic languages. The first type of language has a special focus position which occurs immediately following the verb. All the examples below are taken from Tuller.

(Western Bade)
(10) a. a təla hawə ndi slədə nda.
cook where one meat int
'Where did one cook the meat?'
b. a təla dəʸkwəɓəgə malə slədə.
cook in kitchen mother-my meat
'My mother cooked meat IN THE KITCHEN.'

(Tuller 1992:305)

In the second type of language exemplified below by Tangale, focus constituents occur not immediately after the verb but rather after the direct object. The result becomes ungrammatical if the focus constituent intervenes between the verb and the direct object:

(Tangale)
(11) a. wa patʊ ayaba nuŋ ta luumo dooji?
will buy bananas who at market tomorrow
'Who will buy bananas at the market tomorrow?'
b.*wa patʊ nuŋ ayaba ta luumo dooji?
will buy who bananas at market tomorrow
'Who will buy bananas at the market tomorrow?'

(12) a. wad Billiri nuŋ dooji?
go Billiri who tomorrow
'Who will go to Billiri tomorrow?'

b.*wad nuŋ Billiri dooji?
go who Billiri tomorrow
'Who will go to Billiri tomorrow?'

(13) a. Mela pad k landan tu nuŋ ta luumo?
Mela bought the gown for who at market
'Who did Mela buy the gown for at the market?'
b.*Mela padʊko tu nuŋ landa ta luumo?
Mela bought for who the gown at market
'Who did Mela buy the gown for at the market?'

(Tuller 1992:307)

In all the ungrammatical sentences, the *wh*-words intervene between the verb and the object NP. Tuller points out that the same constraints hold in other languages like Kanakuru and Ngizim, respectively.

(Kanakuru)
(14) a. are lowoi jewoi la lusha.
bury boy-the slave-the in bush
'THE SLAVE buried the boy in the bush.'
b. na dibəre gami mandai?
buy ram-the who
'Who will buy the ram?'
c. kaa nai mandai?
you call who
'Who are you calling?'
d. a wupə-(ro) landai gən shire.
he sold-Cl cloth-the with her
'He sold the cloth TO HER.'

(Tuller 1992:307)

(Ngizim)

(15) a. Taatkə ɗaa-n tai ii magərafcin?
     showed town who to visitors
     'Who showed the town to the visitors?'
  b. ɗəbdə karee-n Audu aa aasək.
     sold goods Audu in market
     'AUDU sold the goods in the market.'

                                          (Tuller 1992:308)

In all the above examples, the well-formed sentences have a structure in which the direct object intervenes between the verb and the focus constituent. In the ill-formed sentences in (11)-(13), the focus appears immediately after the verb. This is schematically represented in (16a, b).

(16) a. V DO FOC (XP)
  b.*V FOC DO

The canonical unfocused word order in the above languages is SVO and becomes VOS when the subject is focused. Note importantly that (16a) is not derived by rightward movement of the focus constituent since a PP complement, which presumably appears inside a VP, follows the focused constituent (cf. example 15a). Assuming the articulated IP structure outlined by Pollock (1989) and Chomsky (1993), the direct object in (16a) may appear outside the VP, possibly in Spec(AgroP). The surface word order can then be derived by Object Shift and verb raising, as is predicted by Holmberg's (1986) generalization. The derivations of (16a, b) are represented in (17a, b).

(17) a. V_i DO FOC [$_{VP}$ t_i]
  b.*V_i FOC DO [$_{VP}$ t_i]

In the well-formed (17a), the focus appears immediately above the VP, while in the ill-formed (17b), the object intervenes between the focus and the VP.

Hence, the contrast between (17a) and (17b) follows from the assumption that the focused position is immediately above the VP.

The above descriptive generalization concerning the position of the focus supports the view that a focused constituent moves to the specifier position of a projection immediately above a VP, which I label Focus Projection. The following is my proposal:

(18)   The Focus Criterion
       A focus operator must be in a Spec-Head configuration within FocP.

The languages discussed above have the structure schematically illustrated below.[2]

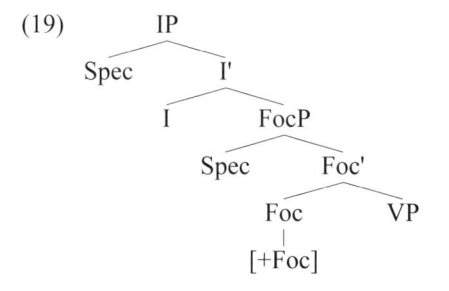

(19)
```
            IP
          /    \
       Spec     I'
              /    \
             I     FocP
                  /    \
               Spec    Foc'
                      /    \
                    Foc    VP
                     |
                   [+Foc]
```

Chomsky (1993) suggests that the strength of Agr features is parameterized. Languages like French have strong Agr features and the verb overtly moves to Infl, whereas English has a weak Agr which prohibits overt movement of the verb. The difference in the position of the focus constituent in the languages illustrated above can then be attributed to the fact that languages differ with

---

[2] A question arises as to how Case is assigned in languages where focus elements move to preverbal position. A problem is that movement from Spec(FocP) to Spec(Agr) results in improper movement and hence must be prohibited. It is worth noting that in many languages, focus constructions are similar to existential constructions such as 'there is a man in the garden' in that Spec (IP) is occupied by an overt expletive. Focused subjects might be assigned Case in a way similar to existential subjects in English. At this point, however, we will leave this issue open to future research.

respect to the position of the verb at S-structure. In languages in which the verb raises to Infl in the overt syntax, the focus constituent appears in a position following the verb. In contrast, in languages in which the verb stays *in-situ* (and possibly raises to Agr at LF), the focus constituent may occur before the verb. In other words, the difference between languages with a preverbal focus position and those with a postverbal focus position may be reduced to differences in the morphological properties of Agr, but not to the position of the focused constituent. The focus constructions of the languages discussed above are now schematically represented as follows:

(20) a. Languages with [Focus+V+O] (i.e. Hungarian)
  [$_{IP}$[$_{FocP}$ FOC [$_{VP}$ V O]]]
 b. Languages with [V+Focus+O] (i.e. Western Bade)
  [$_{IP}$ V$_i$ [$_{FocP}$ FOC [$_{VP}$ t$_i$ O]]]
 c. Languages with [V+O+Focus] (i.e., Tangale, Kanakuru)
  [$_{IP}$ V$_i$ [$_{AgroP}$ O$_j$ [$_{FocP}$ FOC [$_{VP}$ t$_i$ t$_j$]]]]

2.2.4 The Case of Japanese

It is generally assumed that focused constituents in Japanese do not undergo syntactic movement. Contrary to this assumption, this section argues that Japanese, like Hungarian, possesses a unique focus position that appears immediately above a VP.

2.2.4.1 Parallelism Between Noun Phrases and Verb Phrases

It has been argued that the category DP, like other functional categories such as IP and CP, falls under the X' schema and takes a noun phrase as a complement (cf. Chomsky 1986, Tateishi 1994, Watanabe 1992a, and others). Tateishi (1994) argues that case markers instantiate D in Japanese. Hence, (21a) has the structure given in (21b).

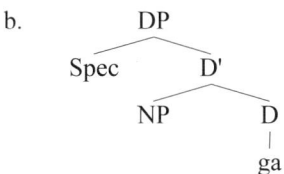

(21) a. Sono otoko-ga kita.
　　　that man-Nom came
　　　'That man came.'
　　b.　　　　　DP
　　　　　　／＼
　　　　　Spec　　D'
　　　　　　　　／＼
　　　　　　　NP　　D
　　　　　　　　　　｜
　　　　　　　　　　ga

Some focus particles such as *dake* 'only' and *made* 'even' can co-occur with structural case markers, in which case the focus particles must precede the case markers. By contrast, focus particles such as *wa, mo* and *sika* may not co-occur with case markers. This is illustrated below.

(22) a. Sono otoko-dake-ga kita.
　　　　that man-only-Nom came
　　b. Sono otoko-sika-*ga ko-na-katta.
　　　　that man-only-*Nom come-not-Past

Due to the fact that some focus particles precede case markers, I assume that noun phrases have the following structure.

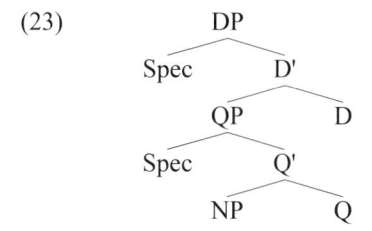

(23)　　　　　DP
　　　　　／＼
　　　　Spec　　D'
　　　　　　　／＼
　　　　　　QP　　D
　　　　　／＼
　　　Spec　　Q'
　　　　　　／＼
　　　　　NP　　Q

Assuming the order of particles given in (22), focus particles such as *dake* appear in Q, while focus particles such as *wa, mo* and *sika* appear in D and hence the latter are in complementary distribution with case markers. Focus particles that appear in a head Q can co-occur not only with a case marker but also with particles in D.

(24) Sono otoko-dake-wa kita.
      that man-only-Foc came
      'Only that man came.'

The following examples illustrate the fact that the focus particles in D block the occurrence of *wh*-words inside a DP.

(25) a. Mary-wa [DP John-no konpyuutaa-no nedan-mo/wa]
        Mary-Top John-Gen computer-Gen price-also/Foc
        siri-tagatteiru.
        know-want
        'Mary wants to know the price of John's computer (also).'
     b. Mary-wa [DP dare-no konpyuutaa-no nedan-o]
        Mary-Top who-Gen computer-Gen price-Acc
        shiri-tagatteiru-no?
        know-want-Q
        'The price of whose computer does Mary want to know?'
     c.*Mary-wa [DP dare-no konpyuutaa-no nedan-mo/wa]
        Mary-Top whose-Gen computer-Gen price-also/Foc
        shiri-tagatteiru-no?
        know-want-Q
        'The price of whose computer (also) does Mary want to know?'

(26) a. [DP John-no Mary-kara-no tegami-mo/wa] todoita.
        John-Gen Mary-from-Gen letter-also/Foc arrived
        'John's letter from Mary (also) has arrived.'
     b. [DP John-no dare-kara-no tegami-ga] todoita-no?
        John-Gen who-from-Gen letter-Nom arrived-Q
        'John's letter from who has arrived?'

c.*[DP John-no dare-kara-no tegami-mo/wa] todoita-no?
John-Gen who-from-Gen letter-also/Foc arrived-Q
'John's letter from who (also) has arrived?'

In (25b) and (26b), where D is marked by Case, island effects are completely absent, while when D is occupied by a focus particle, island effects appear, as shown in (25c) and (26c). In other words, the occurrence of *wh*-words is blocked by a focus element in a head D. A similar pattern exists in English. Consider examples (27a, b).

(27) a. Who bought [John's picture of whom]?
b.?*Who bought [also/even/only John's picture of whom]?

Examples (27a, b) show that in multiple *wh*-questions, a *wh*-word *in-situ* is not allowed inside a DP when the focus particle is present. Assuming that the ill-formed sentences (25c) and (26c) in Japanese are parallel to (27b) in English, I suggest that Spec (DP) in Japanese is occupied by a null expletive operator licensed by a focus particle, as illustrated in (28).

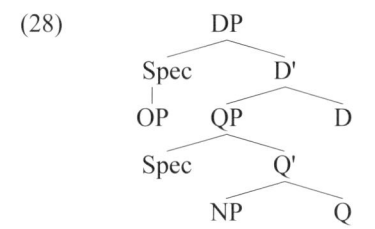

(28)
```
            DP
           /  \
        Spec   D'
         |    /  \
        OP   QP   D
            /  \
         Spec   Q'
               /  \
             NP    Q
```

As in (28), when the null operator is licensed, DP serves as a blocking category for *wh*-words inside it.

It is known that *wh-in-situ* languages with an overt Q-particle exhibit *wh*-island effects:

(29) John-wa [dare-ga nani-o katta-ka] sitteiru-no?
      John-Top who-Nom what-Acc bought Q know-Q
      *'What did John know who bought t ?'
      *'Who did John know what t bought ?'

When (29) is uttered out of the blue, the *wh*-words inside the *wh*-island cannot take different scope and the sentence is acceptable only as a yes-no question. Nishigauchi (1986) shows that *wh*-island effects result from LF movement of *wh*-words. Watanabe (1992b), who assumes that Subjacency is an S-structure constraint, claims that in Japanese, a phonologically empty *wh*-operator originates in *wh-in-situ* and undergoes syntactic movement to Spec(CP). Assuming that *wh*-questions in Japanese involve covert *wh*-movement, the blocking effect as observed in (25c) and (26c) and the *wh*-island effect in (29) is attributable to the following condition:

(30) Minimal Link Condition (MLC)   (Chomsky 1995:311)
      K attracts α only if there is no β, β closer to K than α, such that K attracts β.

According to Chomsky (1995), (30) is regarded as part of the general principle of economy of derivation. If Watanabe's approach is correct in that Japanese involves S-structure *wh*-movement, the MLC prohibits movement of the null *wh*-operator directly to the matrix CP in the configuration given in (31).

(31) *[OP$_i$ ...[$_{DP}$ OP [...t$_i$ ...]]...]

Notice, however, that when an NP is marked by the focus particle *dake*, no island effects are induced. Consider (32a, b):

(32) a. Kimi-wa [_DP_ John-no dono konpyuutaa-no nedan-dake-o]
you-Top John-Gen which computer-Gen price-only-Acc
siri-tai-no?
know-want-Q
'Only the price of which of John's computers do you want to know?'
b. [_DP_ John-no dare-kara-no tegami-dake-ga] todoita-no?
John-Gen who-from-Gen letter-only-Nom arrived-Q
'Only John's letter from who has arrived?'

The well-formed sentences in (32a, b) show that the focus particle *dake* 'only' fails to license the null operator, and hence the *wh*-words are allowed to have matrix scope. Recall that *dake* 'only' is a focus particle that appears in a head Q. This means that the null operator is licensed only under a Spec-Head relation within a DP.

Focus particles such as *wa*, *sae*, and *mo* are not only suffixed to noun phrases but also to verb phrases. These particles appear between the uninflected base form of the verb and the tense morpheme, as illustrated in (33a, b).

(33) a. Kimi-wa [hon-o kai-sae/mo] si-ta.
you-Top book-Acc buy-even/also do-Past
'You even/also read a book.'
b. Kimi-wa [hon-o kau-ka] si-ta.
you-Top book-Acc buy-Q do-Past
'You did something like reading a book.'

When a focus particle is suffixed to a verb, *si* 'do' is inserted between the focus particle and the tense morpheme *ta*. This process is known as a *do*-support.

Given that the presence of a focus particle blocks the occurrence of a *wh*-phrase inside an NP, we can predict that a focus particle attached to the verb behaves in the same way. This prediction is borne out. The suffixation of a focus particle blocks the occurrence of *wh*-words inside a VP.[3] Consider (34).

(34) *Kimi-wa [nani-o kai-sae/mo] si-ta-no?
 you-Top what-Acc buy-even/also-do-Past-Q
 'What did you even/also buy?'

The ill-formedness of (34) is parallel to that of (25c) and (26c), showing that focus particles have a blocking effect on *wh*-words inside a VP. Based on the distribution of focus particles and on this type of evident inner island effect, I hypothesize that verb phrases are parallel to noun phrases, in that a functional category, namely Foc, immediately dominates a VP in Japanese.

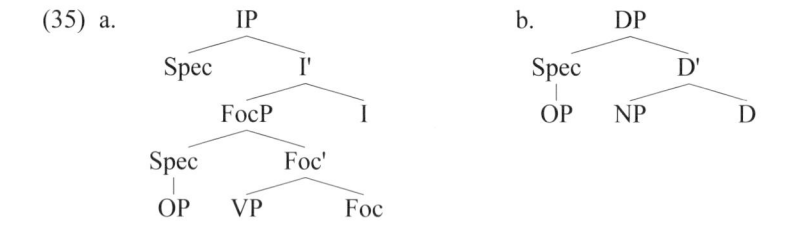

(35) a.
```
        IP
       /  \
     Spec   I'
           /  \
         FocP   I
        /    \
      Spec    Foc'
       |     /   \
       OP   VP   Foc
```

b.
```
        DP
       /  \
     Spec   D'
      |    /  \
      OP  NP   D
```

In both (35a) and (35b), the null operators are licensed by focus particles and block a direct question reading of *wh*-words.

The inner island effects are induced when an NP is marked by a focus particle as in (36a-c).

---

[3] The focus particles that appear in Q, such as *dake* 'only' and *made* 'even', may not be suffixed to the verb even in a sentence containing no *wh*-words.
 (i) *John-wa hon-o kau-dake/made si-ta.
   John-Top book-Acc buy-only/even did
   'John did only/even buy a book.'

(36) a. ?*John-wa Mary-ni-sae nani-o okutta-no?
John-Top Mary-to-even what sent-Q
'What did John send even to Mary?'
b. ?*John-wa Mary-ni-mo nani-o okutta-no?
John-Top Mary-to-also what-Acc sent-Q
'What did John send to Mary also?'
c. ?*John-wa Mary-ni-sika nani-o okura-nak-atta-no?
John-Top Mary-to-only what-Acc send-not-Past-Q
'What did John send only to Mary?'

In (36a-c), the object NPs are marked by the focus particles *sae* 'even', *mo* 'also' and *sika* 'only' respectively. The ill-formed sentences in (36a-c) are represented in (37), in which the morphologically marked element appears in Spec(FocP).[4]

(37) *[$_{CP}$ OP$_i$ ...[$_{FocP}$ DP [$_{VP}$...t$_i$ ...]]]

It is clear that the ill-formedness of (37) is reducible to the MLC as given in (30). FocP serves as an A' position, which blocks the movement of the null *wh*-operator. Note that the above sentences become acceptable when the *wh*-phrase is scrambled out of the VP. This is illustrated in (38a-c).

(38) a. John-wa nani-o Mary-ni-sae okutta-no?
John-Top what Mary-to-even sent-Q
'What did John send even to Mary?'
b. John-wa nani-o Mary-ni-mo okutta-no?
John-Top what-Acc Mary-to-also sent-Q
'What did John send to Mary also?'

---

[4] The NP marked by *dake* does not induce the island effect as in (i).
(i) John-wa Mary-dake-ni nani-o okutta-no?
John-Top Mary-only-to what-Acc sent-Q
'What did John send only to Mary?'
The grammatically of (i) shows that the NP marked by *dake* does not appear in FocP.

c. John-wa nani-o Mary-ni-sika okura-nak-atta-no?
   John-Top what-Acc Mary-to-only send-not-Past-Q
   'What did John send only to Mary?'

It has been widely claimed that clause internal scrambling is movement to a position that has the properties of A positions (cf. Webelhuth 1989, Déprez 1989, Mahajan 1990, Saito 1989, 1992, and others). If clause-internal scrambling is movement to an A position, the acceptability of (38a-c) can be accounted for straightforwardly. FocP as an A' position does not serve as an intervening category for A movement.

2.2.4.2 Distribution of VP Adverbs

Another argument that supports the view that focused constituents appear in Spec(FocP) has to do with the distribution of a certain class of adverbs modifying VPs. Adverbs like *hayaku* 'fast', *matigatte* 'accidentally,' and *yukkuri* 'slowly' are adjoined to a VP. Consider the following examples.

(39) a. John-wa yukkuri wain-o nomu.
       John-Top slowly wine-Acc drink
       'John drinks wine slowly.'
    b. John-wa wain-o yukkuri nomu.
       John-Top wine-Acc slowly drink

The general assumption is that the adverb *yukkuri* 'slowly' is VP-adjoined, and the object *wine* appears *in-situ* in (39a), while in (39b) it is scrambled. The sentence, however, becomes deviant when the adverb appears outside a VP, as shown in the following sentences:[5]

---

[5] In (41), the object NP marked by *wa* is read as having contrastive emphasis.

(40) a. John-wa wain-sae yukkuri nomu.
John-Top wine-even slowly drink
'John drinks even wine slowly.'
b. ?*John-wa yukkuri wain-sae nomu.
John-Top slowly wine-even drink

(41) a. John-wa wain-wa yukkui nomu.
John-Top wine-Foc slowly drink
'John drinks WINE slowly (but not beer).'
b. ?*John-wa yukkuri wain-wa nomu.
John-Top slowly wine-Foc drink

(42) a. John-wa wain-o nihai yukkuri nomu.
John-Top wine-Acc two-glasses slowly drink
'John drinks two glasses of wine slowly.'
b. ?*John-wa yukkuri wain-o nihai nomu.
John-Top slowly wine-Acc two-glasses drink

(43) a. John-wa wain-sika yukkuri noma-nai.
John-Top wine-only slowly drink-not
'John drinks only wine slowly.'
b. ?*John-wa yukkuri wain-sika noma-nai.
John-Top slowly wine-only drink-not

In the ill-formed (b) examples of (40-43), the adverb appears before the focused constituent. The above examples suggest that object NPs marked by a focus particle must appear outside a VP. More examples are given below:

(44) a. John-wa sono tegami-wa hayaku yonda.
John-Top this letter-Foc fast read
'John read THIS LETTER fast (but not that letter).'

b. *John-wa hayaku sono tegami-wa yonda.
John-Top fast this letter-Foc read

(45) a. John-wa tegami-o nanmai-ka hayaku yonda.
John-Top letter-Acc some quickly read
'John read some letters quickly.'

b. ?*John-wa hayaku tegami-o nanmai-ka yonda.
John-Top quickly letter-Acc some read

(46) a. John-wa syoosetsu-sika hayaku yoma-nai.
John-Top novels-only fast read-not
'John read only novels fast.'

b. *John-wa hayaku syoosetsu-sika yoma-nai.
John-Top fast novels-only read-not

(47) a. John-wa sono tegami-sae hayaku yoma-naka-tta.
John-Top this letter-even fast read-not-Past
'John didn't read even this letter fast.'

b. *John-wa hayaku sono tegami-sae yoma-naka-tta.
John-Top fast this letter-even read-not-Past

The sharp contrast between the (a) and (b) examples of (44-47) again supports the idea that object NPs marked by a focus particle appear in a position immediately above the VP.

The adjunct *naze* behaves exactly parallel to focused *wh*-words. Consider (48) and (49).

(48) a. John-ga naze hayaku hon-o yonda-no?
John-Nom why fast book-Acc read-Q
'Why did John read a book fast?'

b. *John-ga hayaku naze hon-o yonda-no?
John-Nom fast why book-Acc read-Q

(49) a. John-ga hayaku nani-o yonda-no?
John-Nom fast what-Acc read-Q
'What did John read fast?'
b. John-ga nani-o hayaku yonda-no?
John-Nom what-Acc fast read-Q

The above examples show that while argument *wh*-words may stay *in-situ*, *naze* 'why' must appear directly in Spec(FocP) on a par with morphologically marked focus phrases. This may suggest that *naze* 'why' is a true operator that is required to be in a Spec-Head relation with a head Foc. Finally, let us consider the following sentences, originally discussed by Saito (1987, 1989).

(50) a. *Kimi-wa naze nani-o katta-no?
you-Top why what-Acc bought-Q
'You bought what why?'
b. Kimi-wa nani-o naze katta-no?
you-Top what-Acc why bought-Q
'You bought why what?'

(51) a. *Naze dare-ga hon-o katta-no?
why who-Nom book-Acc bought-Q
'Who bought a book why?'
b. Dare-ga hon-o naze katta-no?
who-Nom book-Acc why bought-Q

Sentences (50) and (51) show that, in multiple *wh*-questions, naze must appear immediately before the verb. In the (a) examples, *naze* 'why' precedes the argument *wh*-word and in the (b) examples, *naze* follows the argument *wh*-word. Saito (1987) originally argues that the contrast in grammaticality given in (50) and (51) is accounted for by a linear crossing constraint. That is, in multiple *wh*-questions, the *wh*-word that linearly follows others is coindexed with Q, and two lines formed by A' dependencies must not cross at S-structure.

In the (a) examples of (50) and (51), the argument *wh*-word is coindexed with Q to satisfy the linear crossing constraint, but this results in an ECP violation. That is, *naze*, which is not coindexed with Q, is not properly governed by Q, following the Comp indexing mechanism, proposed by Aoun, Hornstein and Sportiche (1981). In the (b) examples of (50) and (51), *naze* is coindexed with Q. An ECP violation does not arise, since the argument *wh*-word is insensitive to the ECP in Japanese.

The proposal that *naze* appears in Spec(FocP), however, provides a straightforward explanation for the contrasts given in (50) and (51) without appeal to the ECP analysis for *naze*. Given that *naze* is a quantificational *wh*-word and appears in Spec(FocP), the grammatical and ungrammatical sentences in (50) and (51) are represented in (52a) and (52b) respectively.

(52) a. [CP [wh$_i$...[FocP naze [VP ...t$_i$...]]]]
    b. *[CP OP$_i$ ...[FocP naze [VP ...t$_i$ wh...]]]

In (52a), the clause internal scrambling of the *wh*-word is not an instance of A' movement, and thus FocP, as an A' position, does not serve as an intervening category. In contrast, (52b) involves covert *wh*-movement, which is blocked by the presence of FocP due to the MLC. The contrast in (52a, b) is accounted for on a par with (36) and (38), repeated in (53a, b).

(53) a. John-wa nani-o Mary-ni-sika okura-nak-atta-no?
        John-Top what-Acc Mary-to-only send-not-Past-Q
        'What did John send only to Mary?'
    b. ?*John-wa Mary-ni-sika nani-o okura-nak-atta-no?
        John-Top Mary-to-only what-Acc send-not-Past-Q
        'What did John send only to Mary?'

The following section focuses on the discussion of indefinite QPs, suggesting that indefinite QPs move to Spec(FocP) in the syntax.

2.3 Indefinites

The existence of an internal operator position has been suggested in the literature. Following the restricted quantifier approach (cf. Lewis 1975, Heim 1982), Diesing (1992) proposes that indefinites are interpreted with respect to an existential closure which is structurally mapped onto the VP-adjoined position. In this section, I will discuss the syntactic properties of indefinite QPs, and claim that the indefinite QP moves to Spec(FocP).

2.3.1 Diesing's (1992) Analysis

Since Heim's (1982) important work, it has been widely assumed that indefinite NPs have no quantificational force by themselves, but rather serve as variables in the logical representation. Their quantificational force comes from other elements such as adverbs of quantification. Heim proposes that quantified sentences have a tripartite logical form that consists of a quantifier, a restrictive clause and a nuclear scope. This is shown below.

(54) a. Every farmer beats a donkey.
 b. Every$_x$ [x is a farmer] ($\exists_y$) y is a donkey & x beats y

Diesing (1992) claims that the logical representation given in (54b) can be derived from the corresponding syntactic structure of the sentence and proposes the mapping hypothesis in (55), which is schematically represented in (56).

(55) The Mapping Hypothesis
 Material from VP is mapped into the nuclear scope.
 Material from IP is mapped into a restrictive clause.

(56)
```
                    IP
              ┌─────┴─────┐
            Spec          IP  ◄─── Restrictive Clause
                    ┌─────┴─────┐
                   Spec         VP
         Nuclear Scope ──► Spec
```

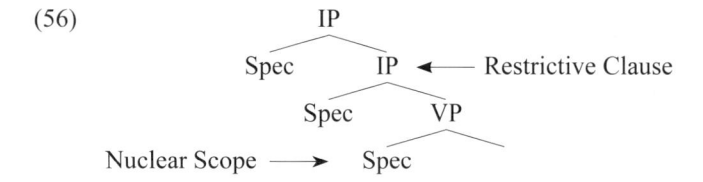

It is known that focusing a constituent divides a sentence into two parts: Presupposition and Focus. Let us consider examples (57a, b).

(57) a. HURRICANES used to arise in this part of the Pacific.
     b. Hurricanes used to arise IN THIS PART OF THE PACIFIC.

In (57a, b), the focused constituents favor an existential reading, whereas the unfocused materials are presupposed and have the flavor of a universal reading. Sentences (57a, b) are mapped onto the different LF structures given in (58a, b).

(58) a. Gen_l [this part of the Pacific (l)] $\exists_x$ [Hurricanes (x) & arise in (x,l)]
     b. Gen_x [Hurricanes(x)] $\exists_l$ [this part of the Pacific (l) & arise in (x,l)]

In (58a, b), Gen refers to an implicit generic quantifier and the binding of variables by Gen results in a generic reading. In both representations, the focused constituents are bound by the existential operator.

   Diesing shows that there are two types of indefinite NPs which behave differently with respect to island effects. When indefinites have an existential reading, extraction out of the NP is possible. In contrast, extraction is not allowed when indefinites have a presuppositional reading. This is shown in the following examples, cited from Diesing.

(59) a. Who do you usually read a book by t?
     b. Who do you usually play a sonata by t?
     c. What do you usually buy a picture of t?
     d. Who do you usually comment on an essay by t?

e. What do you usually publish a book about t?

All the predicates illustrated above allow an existential reading of the indefinite object and extraction out of the NP is possible. Diesing indicates that experiencer predicates allow only a presuppositional reading and extraction of the object is not possible, as shown in (60).

(60) a. *What do you usually like a picture of t?
　　 b. *Who do you usually love a sonata by t?
　　 c. *What do you usually appreciate a good joke about t?
　　 d. *What do you usually hate an article about t?
　　 e. *Who do you generally detest an opera by t?
　　 f. *What do you generally abhor a book about t?
　　 h. *Who do you generally despise a painting of t?
　　 i. *Who/what do you generally loathe a story about t?

In all the above examples, an existential reading of the object is not available, and hence extraction of the object is ruled out. Diesing claims that indefinites with an existential reading are construed as non-quantificational variables and stay inside the VP, whereas indefinites with a presuppositional reading have a quantificational force of their own. The former receive existential force from existential closure, while the latter must undergo QR and form an operator-variable structure. Diesing proposes the following condition:

(61)　Extraction Constraint
　　　Extraction cannot take place out of an NP that must raise out of VP.

Diesing argues that extraction out of an NP that itself undergoes movement creates a configuration which violates Subjacency.[6] Since the indefinite NPs in (60) undergo QR, *wh*-movement out of the NPs violates the Extraction

---

[6] Diesing assumes that Subjacency is a condition on representations.

Constraint in (61).

The condition stated in (61) is, however, descriptively inadequate. Lasnik and Saito (1992) argue that extraction from constituents in A-bar positions gives sentences with only a marginal status. The following are examples cited by Lasnik and Saito(1992).

(62) a. I think that you should read [$_{NP}$ articles about vowel harmony] carefully.
   b. I think that [$_{NP}$ articles about vowel harmony] you should read t carefully.
   c. ??Vowel harmony, I think that [$_{NP}$ articles about t] you should read t carefully.

In (62b) the NP *articles about vowel harmony* has been topicalized to the IP-adjoined position. In (62c), the NP *vowel harmony* is topicalized to the matrix IP position from the NP that is itself topicalized. (62c) is only marginal. Lasnik and Saito argue that (62c) should not be excluded by Subjacency. Now consider sentences (63a, b).

(63) a. ?*Who do you think that [$_{NP}$ pictures of t] are on sale?
   b. ??Who do you think that [$_{NP}$ pictures of t] John wanted t?

(63a) is a violation of Subjacency. If (63b) does violate Subjacency, we expect this example to be ungrammatical; i.e. to have the same status as (63a). However, the grammaticality of (63b) is the same as that of (62c) and is clearly better than that of (63a). Lasnik and Saito conclude that (63b) does not violate Subjacency but that its marginality is due to the "internal constituent effect."

In the following discussion, I hypothesize that FocP is instantiated in English when a quantificational element is present and that it moves to Spec(FocP) at LF. The structure is represented in (64).

(64)
```
            CP
           /  \
        Spec   C'
              /  \
             C    IP
                 /  \
              Spec   I'
                    /  \
                   I    FocP
                       /    \
                    Spec    Foc'
                           /   \
                         Foc    VP
```

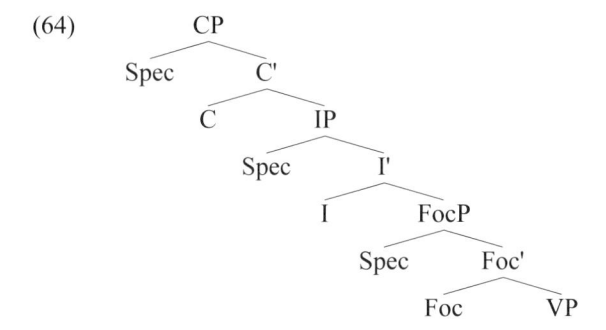

The idea that Spec(FocP) is an intermediate landing site for *wh*-words will be discussed in greater depth in the next chapter. A stipulation at this point is that the sentences in (60) are not possible since *wh*-movement in English leaves a trace in Spec(FocP) and this trace blocks the LF movement of the indefinite NP. The non-quantificational indefinites in (59), on the other hand, do not involve movement at all, yielding well-formed structures.

The clause internal operator position is further supported by Diesing's (1992) observations concerning indefinite NPs in German, as illustrated below (Diesing 1992:119).

(65) a. ...daß Hilda immer [$_{NP}$ Sonaten von Dittersdorf] spielt.
       that Hilda always   sonatas by Dittersdorf play
       '...that Hilda is always playing sonatas by Dittersdorf.'
   b. ...daß Hilda [$_{NP}$ Sonaten von Dittersdorf] immer spielt.
       that Hilda   sonatas by Dttersdorf   always play
       'If it is a sonata by Dittersdorf, Hilda plays it.'

In (65a), the object is VP-internal, while in (65b) the object is scrambled out of the VP. According to Diesing, the unscrambled indefinite yields an existential interpretation, while the scrambled indefinite object receives a quantificational interpretation. What Diesing attempts to show is that quantificational indefinites in English move at LF, while those in German move at S-structure. The fact that the landing site for this movement is between the subject and the VP lends support to the existence of the internal operator position in German, as well. Diesing points out that *wh*-movement out of an NP is not possible from the scrambled NP, while it is possible from the unscrambled NP, as illustrated as below.

(66) a. Was_i hat Hilda immer [NP t_i für Sonaten] gespielt?
     What has Hilda always   for sonatas played
     'What kind of sonatas did Hilda always play.'
   b. *Was_i hat Hilda [NP t_i für Sonaten] immer gespielt?
     What has Hilda   for sonatas   always played

Suppose that *wh*-movement in German employs a clause internal FocP. (66a) is acceptable in that the *wh*-word moves to CP successive-cyclically through FocP. In (66b), the trace of the *wh*-word is left behind in Spec(FocP), which blocks the remnant movement of the NP.

In the following section, I will explore the interaction between quantificational indefinites and *wh*-words in other languages, suggesting that both types of elements move to Spec(FocP).

2.3.2 Interaction between Indefinites and *Wh*-Words

Indefinites and *wh*-words in many languages are morphologically related. Languages may be divided into three groups. In the first group, the interrogative versions of *wh*-words appear in a bare form, while the indefinite versions are derived by either prefixing or suffixing certain particles to the bare form. The following languages belong to this type.

(67)

		Wh-words	Indefinites
Japanese		dare ('who')	dare-ka ('someone')
		nani ('what')	nani-ka ('something')
Hungarian		ki ('who')	vala-ki ('someone')
		mi ('what')	vala-mi ('something')

(67) shows that, in both Japanese and Hungarian, indefinites are derived from *wh*-words with Q-particles, which are suffixed in Japanese and are prefixed in Hungarian.

Languages like Chinese and Korean exhibit no such morphological alternation. Indefinites in these languages employ a bare *wh*-word without a Q-particle affixed to it.

(68)

	Wh-words	Indefinites
Mandarin Chinese	shui ('who')	shui ('someone')
	shenme ('what')	shenme ('something')
Korean	nwukwu ('who')	nwukwu ('someone')
	mues ('what')	mues ('something')

As shown in (68), neither a *wh*-word nor an indefinite is attached to a Q-particle in Chinese or Korean. Finally, the third group includes earlier Japanese and Sinhala. In those languages, both *wh*-words and indefinites have the same form, consisting of a bare *wh*-word with a Q-particle attached to it.

(69)

	Wh-words	Indefinites
Earlier Japanese	dare-ka ('who')	dare-ka ('someone')
	nani-ka ('what')	nani-ka ('something')
Sinhala	kauru-də ('who')	kauru-də ('someone')
	mokak-də ('what')	mokak-də ('something')

It has been pointed out that languages like Japanese and Korean restrict the co-occurrence of indefinites and *wh*-words. Hoji (1985) has observed that in Japanese, sentences with the order [∃, WH] are not acceptable. Hoji gives the following examples:

(70) a. ?*John-ka Bill-ga nani-o nonda-no?
John or Bill-Nom what-Acc drank-Q
'What did John or Bill drink?'
b. ??Dareka-ga nani-o nonda-no?
someone-Nom what-Acc drank-Q
'What did someone drink?'

Kim (1989) has reported the same pattern in Korean as well. The following examples are from Kim:

(71) Nwu-ka mues-ul kajewat ni?
WH/QP-Nom WH/QP-Acc brought-Q
(i) 'Who brought what?'
(ii) 'Did someone bring something?'
(iii) 'Who brought something?'
(iv) *'What did someone bring?' (Kim 1989)

Sentence (71) allows the three interpretations given in (i)-(iii). But, parallel to Japanese, what is not allowed is the reading (iv) with the surface [∃, WH] order. Recall that *wh*-words and focus elements show exactly the same contrast. The examples are given in (72).

(72) a. ?*John-sae nani-o yonda-no?
John-even what-Acc read-Q
'What did even John read ?'
b. ?*John-mo nani-o yonda-no?
John-also what-Acc read-Q
'What did John also read ?'

The parallelism in acceptability between focus elements and indefinites shows that indefinites are treated on a par with focus elements, in that they move to the clause-internal operator position, namely Spec(FocP) in the overt syntax.

Finally, Hoji (1985) indicates that a universal quantifier marked by the particle *mo* behaves syntactically like an existential quantifier. A universal quantifier in Japanese consists of a *wh*-word with the Q-particle *mo* attached to it. As is also the case in English, the wide scope reading of *daremo* 'everyone' is not available as shown in (73).

(73) Dare-ga daremo-o syootai sita-no?
      who-Nom everyone-Acc invited-Q
      'Who invited everyone?'

Hoji points out that (74) is possible only if *daremo* 'everyone' has a "group" reading.

(74) Daremo-ga nani-o katta-no?
      everyone-Nom what-Acc bought-Q
      'What did everyone buy?'

(74) is grammatical as a question asking for the identity of the things that everyone in question bought. Thus the felicitous answer must be a single constituent answer, such as 'They bought wine'. Unlike the English counterpart, (74) does not admit a pair-list answer such as 'John bought wine, Sue bought beer and Bill bought cola.' Thus, if we force a distributive reading on *daremo* 'everyone', by adding *sorezore*, 'each, individually', the sentence becomes unacceptable.[7]

(75) *Daremo-ga sorezore nani-o katta-no?
      everyone-Nom each what-Acc bought-Q
      'What did everyone each buy?'

The ungrammaticality of (75) shows that *daremo* 'everyone' does not have wide

---

[7] The judgment is Hoji's (1985).

scope over *nani* 'what'. Under our analysis, the fact that (75) is not permissible may suggest that *daremo* with a distributional reading is treated on a par with focus elements in that it appears in Spec(FocP). The position of VP adverbs further supports the view that universal QPs undergo syntactic movement to Spec(FocP). Consider examples (76) and (77).

(76) a. John-wa doremo-o matigatte katta.
John-Top everything-Acc mistakenly bought
'John mistakenly bought everything.'
b. John-wa doremo-o yoku tsukau.
John-Top everything-Acc often use
'John often uses everything.'

(77) a. John-wa matigatte doremo-o katta.
John-Top mistakenly everything-Acc bought
b. John-wa yoku doremo-o tsukau.
John-Top often everything-Acc use

Sentences (76) and (77) differ in the position of the VP adverb. Although (76) and (77) are both acceptable, they have different meanings. The universal quantifier *doremo* in (76) allows both a distributive and a group reading, whereas in (77) it allows only a group reading. The contrast is sharper in the (b) examples of (76) and (77). The adverb *yoku* 'often' quantifies over events. Suppose that John has three pens. (76b) may mean that John uses one pen per one event. It can also be interpreted with a group reading, in which case John uses all three pens per one event. (77b), however, allows only a group reading. The difference in meaning indicates that *doremo* with the distributive reading moves to the clause-internal operator position.

In this section, I have discussed the interaction between *wh*-words and focus elements, suggesting that *wh*-questions in Japanese involve covert *wh*-movement and that FocP serves as an intervening category for *wh*-movement. Spec(FocP) is a potential landing site for *wh*-movement; hence, if a focus element occupies FocP, a violation of the Minimal Link Condition (MLC) results.

2.4 The Focus Marker *Ittai*

In this section, I will discuss some syntactic characteristics of the focus marker *ittai* in Japanese, showing that *ittai* behaves like a quantificational operator and that it appears in either CP or FocP.

Pesetsky (1987) notes that *ittai* behaves similarly to the word 'the hell' in English. *Ittai*, however, differs from 'the hell' in English in that the former has little semantic meaning other than simply adding a focus reading to a *wh*-phrase in its scope. I suggest that *ittai* behaves like a Q-expletive in languages shown in Chapter 1; for example, Egyptian Arabic as illustrated in (78a, b):

(78) a. Hiyya Mona raahit feen?
 Q Mona went where?
 b. Hiyya Mona xaragit?
 Q Mona leave?

(Wahba 1984:120)

The expletive *hiyya* in Egyptian Arabic can be used in both *wh*-questions and yes-no questions as illustrated in (78a, b). The word *ittai* is an adverb associated with *wh*-words and non-interrogative focus words in yes-no questions, but not in non-interrogative sentences. This is illustrated in (79a-c).

(79) a. John-wa ittai nani-o katta-no?
 John-Top OP what-Acc bought-Q
 'What is it that John bought?'
 b. John-wa ittai **hon-o** katta-no?
 John-Top OP book-Acc bought-Q
 'Did John buy BOOKS?'

c. *John-wa ittai **hon-o** katta.
   John-Top OP book-Acc bought
   'John bought BOOKS.'

The fact that *ittai* can be associated with *wh*-phrases and non-interrogative focus elements in yes-no questions shows that *ittai* behaves like a Q-expletive. The word *ittai* and the associated focused element need not be adjacent. In fact, the dependency between *ittai* and *wh*-words can be unbounded. Thus, the following sentences are completely acceptable.

(80) a. John-wa ittai$_i$ kinoo honya-de nani-o$_i$ katta-no?
     John-Top OP yesterday bookstore-Loc what-Acc bought-Q
     'What is it that John bought in the bookstore yesterday?'
   b. John-wa ittai$_i$ Mary-ni [dare-ga$_i$ kaita hon-o] kasita-no?
      John-Top OP Mary-Dat who-Nom wrote book-Acc lent-Q
      '*Who is it that John lent Mary a book that wrote?'

The dependency between *ittai* and *wh*-phrases, however, obeys *wh*-island conditions.

(81) *John wa ittai$_i$ Sue-ni [Mary ga nani-o$_i$ katta-ka]
      John-Top OP Sue-Dat Mary-Nom what-Acc bought Q
      tazuneta-no?
      asked-Q
      'Did John ask Sue what it is that Mary bought?'

(81) is excluded because *ittai* cannot bind the *wh*-phrase inside the *wh*-island. The ungrammaticality given in (81) is attributable to the MLC.

Another characteristic of *ittai* is that it behaves like a focus phrase in that it must appear before a VP adverb. This is shown in (82) and (83).

(82) a. John-wa ittai nani-o yoku kau-no?
John-Top OP what-Acc often buy-Q
'What is it that John bought often?'
b. ?*John-wa yoku ittai nani-o kau-no?
John-Top often OP what-Acc buy-Q

(83) a. John-wa ittai nani-o hayaku nonda-no?
John-Top OP what-Acc fast drank-Q
'John drank what fast?'
b. ?*John-wa hayaku ittai nani-o nonda-no?
John-Top fast OP what-Acc drank-Q

A sharp contrast indicated in (82) and (83) shows that *ittai* appears in a position outside a VP, namely Spec(FocP). Furthermore, in multiple *wh*-questions all the *wh*-words within the scope of *ittai* must be focused, as shown in (84a, b).

(84) John-wa ittai$_{i, j}$ [kinoo nani-o$_i$ doko-de$_j$ katta]-no?
John-Top OP yesterday what-Acc where-Loc bought-Q
'What did John buy where yesterday?'

Given that *ittai* is a Q-adverb which has a quantificational force of its own, I propose that *ittai* is treated as an overt polyadic *wh*-operator with the complex features [+Foc, +Q], and unselectively binds *wh*-words in its c-command domain. The fact that *ittai* and *wh*-words exhibit the *wh*-island effect shows that at least one of the *wh*-words in multiple *wh*-questions involve movement, as is the case in multiple *wh*-questions in languages with overt *wh*-movement.

In this chapter, I have provided a number of arguments supporting the existence of an internal operator projection, which I label Focus Projection. Morphologically marked focused elements appear in Spec(FocP) and this position serves as a blocking category for both overt and covert *wh*-movement. The MLC accounts for a wide range of syntactic constraints in Japanese.

3

Clitic Q-Movement

3.1 Introduction

I argued in Chapter 2 that not only Japanese but also languages like English and German employs a clause internal operator position FocP, and that quantificational indefinites move to this position either covertly or overtly. This position is also used as an intermediate landing site for *wh*-movement in these languages. Assuming that *wh*-movement involves an interaction between a *wh*-feature and a Q-feature (cf. Chomsky 1995), in this chapter I argue that a Q-feature realized as *ka* in Japanese is a clitic base-adjoined to Foc, and that it undergoes head movement to Comp. I call this clitic Q-movement

In English, *wh*-movement of non-subjects is accompanied by Subject-Auxiliary Inversion (SAI), in which inflected auxiliaries precede subjects. Since Chomsky's (1986) work, SAI is represented as a type of structure-preserving I-to-C movement. Germanic languages other than English, in general, exhibit Verb Second phenomena, in which a finite verb moves to Comp. Rizzi (1991) suggests that SAI is a special case of Verb Second, which he labels "residual V2." Let us consider the following examples in English, Dutch and German.

(1) a. What has Peter read?
   b. Hvad har Peter lust?
   c. Was hat Peter gelesen?

In all the interrogative sentences in (1) the inflected auxiliary verb moves to Comp. In Japanese, a Comp is occupied by a Q-particle, as illustrated in (2).

(2)   Dare-ga ki-masita-ka?
      who-Nom come-Aux-Q
      'Who came?'

It is widely assumed that a Q-particle is a morphological realization of [+Q] features and that it originates in Comp (cf. Nishigauchi 1986, Cheng 1991). Chomsky (1995) introduces the concept of the strength of a feature and proposes that:

(3)   If F is strong, then F is a feature of a nonsubstantive category and F is checked by a categorial feature.

Feature strength determines language variations. A strong feature triggers an overt movement to eliminate it by checking. I argue that in both types of *wh*-interrogatives, as illustrated above, [+Q] features are strong, and that they are base-generated in Foc and move to Comp in the overt syntax.

I will examine a wide range of syntactic phenomena, including I-to-C movement in English, V2 effects in the Germanic languages, and root-embedded and subject-object asymmetries in various languages. It will be shown that the clitic Q-movement hypothesis gives a unified account for what otherwise appears to be language-particular phenomena.

3.2 Head Movement

Many proposals have been provided in order to account for such phenomena as subject-Aux inversion in English and verb second effects in Germanic languages. In all instances, head movement has been considered strictly local. Thus, raising a second Aux to Comp or moving V across Aux yields an ungrammatical sentence, as shown in the following examples.

(4) a. Has he been fixing the car?
    b. *Been he has fixing the car?
    c. *Fixed he has the car?

The locality constraint on head movement seen in (4) is expressed by the well-known constraint proposed in Travis (1984).

(5)   Head Movement Constraint (Travis 1984)
    An X^0 may only move into the Y^0 that selects the maximal projection of X^0.

In short, (5) predicts that movement of V to Comp is possible only if it first moves to Infl. Movement of V directly to Comp bypassing an intervening Infl is prohibited.

3.2.1 V-to-I Movement

A verb has a set of inflectional features (Tense/Agr) in the lexicon, which must be checked against the Agr position. Overt V-to-I movement is induced if and only if the language in question has strong Agr. The parametric difference between English and French with respect to V-to-I movement is attested to by the position of VP-adverbials such as *often*.

(6) a. John often kisses Mary.
b. *John kisses often Mary.

(7) a. John completely lost his mind.
b. *John lost completely t his mind.

(8) a. Jean embrasse souvent Marie.
b. *Jean souvent embrasse Marie.

(9) a. Jean perdit complètement la tete.
b. *Jean complètement perdit la tete.

In French, in contrast to English, a VP adverbial cannot precede a verb. It therefore follows that French induces overt V-to-I movement, whereas English does not do so in the overt syntax. In Chomsky (1993), French-type languages have "strong" Agr, which forces overt raising of the verb, while English-type languages have "weak" Agr, which blocks verb raising in syntax.

3.2.2 I-to-C Movement

In English, I-to-C movement is obligatory in *wh*-questions of non-subjects, as given in (10).

(10) What has Peter read?

Rizzi (1991) suggests that in (10), [+Wh] is licensed in Infl, and that I-to-C movement is triggered by the following principle.

(11) The *Wh*-Criterion (Rizzi 1991)
a. A *wh*-operator must be in a Spec-head configuration with an $X^0_{[+Wh]}$.
b. An $X^0_{[+Wh]}$ must be in a Spec-head configuration with a *wh*-operator.

(11) states that at some level of representation, the *wh*-operator must be in the

specifier position and [+Wh] in its head position. The only possible structural position where [+Wh] stands in a Spec-head relation is the domain of CP. The *Wh*-criterion ensures that a *wh*-operator is moved to Spec(CP), and that Infl carrying [+Wh] is moved to Comp, as represented in (12).

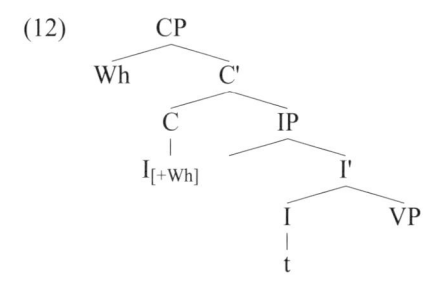

(12)
```
         CP
        /  \
      Wh    C'
           /  \
          C    IP
          |   /  \
       I[+Wh] I'
              /  \
             I    VP
             |
             t
```

Using minimalist terminology, (11) is rephrased as in (13):

(13)   [+Wh] features must be checked against Comp.

Notice, however, that I-to-C movement is not invoked in English when a *wh*-phrase originates in the subject position, as illustrated below.

(14) a. [CP Who [IP t left early]]?
      b. *[CP Who did [IP t leave early]]?

While in (10), I-to-C movement is obligatory, in (14) it is prohibited. There have been many attempts to account for the lack of I-to-C movement in examples like (14) within the theory of the ECP. Rizzi (1990a, 1991) attempts to account for the subject-object asymmetry by appealing to proper head government. Rizzi proposes to reduce the ECP to proper head government as given in (15).

(15)   ECP
       A trace must be properly head-governed.

An object trace is properly head-governed by V, and hence never induces an ECP violation. (14b), however, is ruled out as a violation of the ECP. Under Rizzi's analysis, a head Comp is inert for government in English, and Infl in Comp does not have features rich enough to be a proper governor. It follows that the subject trace in (14b) is not properly head-governed. The subject trace in (14a), on the other hand, is properly governed by the [+Wh] in Comp instantiated by agreement. Rizzi assumes that agreement falls under either a Spec-head configuration or under coindexation. The *Wh*-Criterion is, then, interpreted to include both types of agreement. *Wh*-specification in (14a) is instantiated by the latter type of agreement. That is, the subject trace is coindexed with Infl and *who*; *who* is then coindexed with Comp and, by transitivity, Infl and Comp are coindexed, as illustrated in (16).

(16) [$_{CP}$ Wh$_i$ [C$_i$ [$_{IP}$ t$_i$ [I$_i$ ...]]]]

There have been a number of proposals on *that*-trace effects, which exhibit a subject-object asymmetry in English. Consider (17a, b).

(17) a. Who do you think t left early?
     b. *Who do you think that t left early?

Under Rizzi's account, the embedded Comp can be realized as either 'that' or Agr.

(18) C $\rightarrow$ that
             Agr $_{[+Wh]}$

The [+Wh] in Comp is instantiated not by I-to-C movement, but by a Spec-head relation. Comp, which is inert for government, then becomes an appropriate head governor for the subject trace. (17a) is well formed since the subject trace is licensed by [+Wh] in Comp. By contrast, 'that' prevents a Spec-head agreement and further is inert for government. Hence, (17b) leads to a violation of the ECP. Rizzi's *wh*-specification is summarized in (19):

(19)
	Subjects	Non-Subjects
Matrix Clauses	Coindexation	Free Licensing
Embedded Clauses	Spec-Head Agreement	

Rizzi's analyses provide a unified account for subject-object asymmetries found in root clauses and embedded clauses.

(20) a. Who t left early?
  b. Who did John think t left early?

(21) a. *Who did t leave early?
  b. *Who did John think that t left early?

The sentences in (20) are grammatical because Comp is specified as [+Wh] by agreement; (20a) by coindexation and (20b) by the Spec-head relation. In both cases, the subject trace is properly head-governed. The sentences in (21), however, are ungrammatical, since no agreement relation holds between the specifier and its head within CP.

While the embedded Comp in English blocks I-to-C movement, there are many languages which require inversion even in embedded clauses. For example, in Spanish, subjects cannot intervene between *wh*-elements and inflected verbs either in main or in embedded clauses, and hence the following are ungrammatical.

(22) a. *Que Marie compro?
  'What Marie bought?'
  b. *No se que Marie compro.
  'I don't know what Marie bought.' (Rizzi 1991)

Rizzi (1991) suggests that variations among languages are accounted for by the parameterization of free licensing of [+Wh]. In English, [+Wh] is freely licensed in the matrix Infl, whereas in Spanish [+Wh] is uniformly specified in Infl.

3.2.3 Verb Second

All of the Germanic languages except for English have Verb Second (V2) effects, which consist of movement of a finite verb to the second position of a clause. Most of the generative literature on V2 (cf. den Besten 1983, Thiersch 1978, Taraldsen 1986, Holmberg 1988, and Tomaselli 1990) assumes that a finite verb in German appears in Comp, where a complementizer would otherwise have appeared. Consider the following examples cited from Vikner (1990).

(23) a. The children saw the film.
     b. Die Kinder sahen den Film.

It has been argued that (23a) and (23b) have different structures, as represented by the following trees.

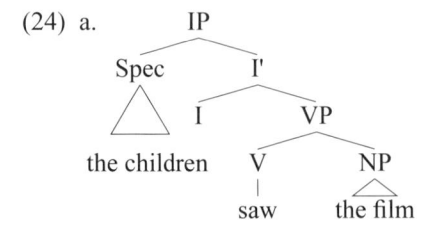

(24) a.
```
              IP
             /  \
          Spec   I'
          /\    /  \
             the children  I    VP
                               /  \
                              V    NP
                              |    /\
                             saw  the film
```

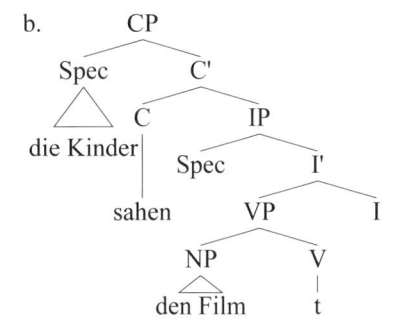

b.
```
           CP
         /    \
      Spec     C'
      /\     /    \
     /  \   C      IP
    die Kinder   /    \
         |     Spec    I'
        sahen        /    \
                    VP     I
                   /  \
                  NP   V
                 /\    |
               den Film t
```

A question that arises is why the verb in German has to move to Comp at all. In other words, what are the morphological motivations for a subject to move to Spec(CP), or for a verb to move to Comp?

As in the case of I-to-C movement, no verb second effect is invoked within embedded clauses. The following examples in Dutch illustrate the point.

(25) Ik heb een huis met een tuintje gehuurd.
      I have a house with a garden rented
      'I rented a house with a little garden.'

(26) a. *dat ik heb een huis met een tuintje gehuurd.
        that I have a house with a little garden rented
     b. dat ik een huis met een tuintje gehuurd heb.

Whereas a finite verb in the matrix clause moves to Comp, this movement is prohibited in the embedded clause since the Comp position is occupied by the complementizer. Thus, there is no target for verb movement.
The complementary distribution between a lexical complementizer and a finite verb is attested in German. The examples are cited from Zwart (1993).

(27) a. Johann glaubt, dass er Maria immer noch liebt.
        John   thinks that he Mary still   loves

b. *Johann glaubt, dass er liebt Maria immer noch.
John thinks that he loves Mary still

(27b) shows that V2 is blocked by the presence of the complementizer. In both German and Danish, verb movement is not only blocked by the presence of the lexical complementizer, but is also blocked in embedded questions. Consider the following examples from Vikner (1990).

(German)
(28) a. Ich weiß nicht, welchen film die Kinder gesehen haben.
         I   know not which   film the children have   seen.
     b. *Ich weiß nicht, welchen film haben die Kinder gesehen.
         I   know not which   film have the children seen.

(Danish)
(29) a. Jeg ved ikke hvilken film bornene har set.
         I know not which film the children have seen.
     b. *Jeg ved ikke hvilken film har bornene set.
         I know not which film have the children seen.

In (28) and (29), the embedded Comp contains the feature [+Wh] in order to satisfy the selectional requirement of the matrix verb. The ungrammaticality of (28b) and (29b) indicates that V2 is blocked by [+Wh] features in Comp. In German, if the Comp selected by the bridge verb contains no lexical complementizer, V2 is obligatory, as illustrated in the following examples.

(30) a. *Johann glaubt, er Maria liebt immer noch.
         John thinks he Mary loves still
     b. Johann glaubt, er liebt Maria immer noch.
         John thinks he loves Mary still

(31) a. *Er sagt, die Kinder diesen Film gesehen haben.
   He says the children this film seen have
b. Er sagt, die Kinder haben diesen Film gesehen.
   He says the children have this film seen

The contrast between the (a) and (b) examples of (30) and (31) shows that V2 is enforced when Comp is empty.

An obvious theoretical question arises as to the motivation of V2. In other words, what forces V to move to Comp at all? Furthermore, how is this morphological requirement satisfied when movement to Comp is not available? Zwart (1993) claims that in non-interrogatives in Germanic languages, some element is forced to move to Spec (CP) if it contains "topic" features (See also Travis 1984). According to Zwart, topics and *wh*-elements by assumption have a [+OP] feature in addition to their Case/agreement features. The PF-visible [+OP] feature in Comp triggers verb movement in main clauses. A verb does not move to Comp in an embedded clause since the presence of a complementizer allows the elimination of this feature. As Zwart (1993: 307) puts it, "The only explanation can be that this PF-visible feature is not directly associated with the finite verb, but with C, and that lexicalization of C suffices for checking and elimination of that feature."[1]

There have been a number of other proposals in relation to V2 effects which are all based on assumptions about the nature of Comp. These include: (1) a Comp must have the feature [+V] (Taraldsen 1986, Holmberg 1988) and (2) a Comp has some features which in non-V2 languages are only found in Infl, such as the feature [+Nom] (Koopman 1984 and Platzack 1986), the feature [+I] (Rizzi 1990b), the feature [+F] (Holmberg and Platzack 1991), the features of tense and agreement (Tomaselli, 1990), the feature of topic (Zwart 1993), and ϕ-features (Law 1991). All these analyses are based on the assumption that

---

[1] Law (1991), on the other hand, proposes that V-movement takes place at LF in embedded clauses. Under his analysis, a complementizer is treated as an expletive, inherently specified for ϕ-features. It must therefore be replaced at LF by non-distinct ϕ-features in order to satisfy the Principle of Full Interpretation.

V2 effects are motivated by some feature (s) of Comp not found in non-V2 languages.

3.3 The Clitic Q-Movement Hypothesis

The idea that V2 is motivated by the feature of Comp, however, raises some theoretical questions concerning the morphologically-driven movement hypothesis. Recall that Chomsky's "last resort" condition states that movement of α is triggered only by the morphological needs of the element α in question. According to this assumption, movement can take place only in order to satisfy the morphological requirements of the moved element itself. The movement of V to satisfy the properties of Comp clearly violates the self-serving "last resort" condition.[2] Following Zwart (1993), I assume that Verb Second is motivated by the presence of a [+Top] feature. Under my analysis, however, a verb is forced to move to Comp only if it "picks up" [+Top] features at an earlier stage in the derivation. As in the case of other functional features, a feature generated in Foc is either strong or weak, depending on the morphological properties of a given language. In other words, V2 languages have a strong [+Top] feature, which is forced to move to Comp to be eliminated by checking. In my account, Q refers to operator features of any kind generated in Foc and Verb Second is induced by Q-movement.

3.3.1 Two Types of Head Movement
Following Rizzi and Roberts (1989) and Roberts (1991, 1993), I assume that there are three types of head movement: 1) free substitution, 2) selected substitution, and 3) adjunction. In the case where X^0 moves to Y^0 and forms an amalgam of morphological complex $[X^0+Y^0]$ (i.e., as in V-to-I movement),

---
[2] Chomsky (2000), however, discards the principle of Greed—"the self-serving last resort" driven by the properties of a moved element. He instead proposes that movement be driven by the uninterpretable feature of the target (i.e., probe), which he refers to as "Suicidal Greed."

the incorporation host morphologically subcategorizes for the incorporee, and hence a structural slot is created at D-structure as a landing site for the incorporee. This is an instance of selected substitution. Roberts proposes that the incorporation trigger is X^{-1} and that the subcategorization frame [+Y___] is base generated within X^0. Selected substitution and adjunction are schematically illustrated as follows.

(32) a. Selected Substitution

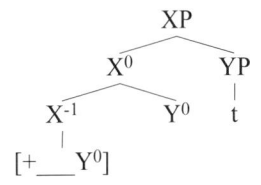

```
              XP
            /    \
          X⁰      YP
         /  \      |
       X⁻¹   Y⁰    t
        |
      [+__Y⁰]
```

b. Adjunction

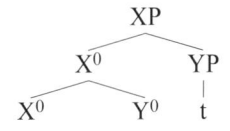

```
              XP
            /    \
          X⁰      YP
         /  \      |
        X⁰   Y⁰    t
```

Roberts attempts to account for the constraints on head movement in terms of the Minimality Condition. If head movement is an instance of selected substitution, excorporation is not possible since it leads to a violation of the Minimality Condition. Excorporation, however, is possible if head movement is an instance of adjunction.

Interpreting Roberts' analysis from a minimalist standpoint, I assume that substitution is analyzed as an instance of morphological checking that takes place between the host and the incorporee. In other words, if X subcategorizes for Y, this means that Y's features are checked off against X, forcing Y to raise to a subcategorization slot created within X. Once the incorporee moves to the slot, the excorporation of Y results in a violation of the following "last resort" principle:

(33) Movement is driven by morphological necessity only.

In the case of adjunction, however, excorporation does not lead to a violation of (33). In other words, long head movement (LHM) of a head X is possible unless the intervening head Y is a potential landing site for X. This is consistent with the view that the HMC, as given in (5) is reduced to the MLC in Chomsky (1995). I argue that Q is a clitic base-adjoined to a functional head. The clitic Q is either overt or covert (i.e., a null clitic) depending on the language. I suggest that Q must satisfy a general property associated with clitic movement; that is, a clitic ends up in a position that provides morphological support. This is attributed to the following condition, originally proposed by Lasnik (1981):

(34) Stranded Affix Filter
An affix must be a syntactic dependent of a morphologically realized category at surface structure.

The next section discusses the syntactic properties of clitic movement found in many languages.

3.3.2 Clitic Movement

Many attempts have been provided to account for the fact that clitics are generally allowed to move across intermediate heads (cf. Baker 1988, Pollock 1989, Li 1990, Belletti 1990, Kayne 1991, Roberts 1991). Let us first look at the well-known examples of clitic movement in French.

(35) a. Jean n'aime pas Marie.
b. *Jean ne pas aime Marie.

Pollock (1989) proposes that the negative adverb *pas* and the head *ne* originate in the specifier and the head of a functional projection NegP respectively. Under Pollock's analysis, the head *ne* is considered to be a clitic that left-adjoins to Agr. The surface word order is derived by leaving the negative adverb in its base position in Spec(NegP) and by moving the negative head *ne* to Agr. Since V in French must move to Agr, *ne* always precedes the inflected verb in Agr position, as illustrated in (36).

(36) a. [AgrP [NegP pas [Neg ne [VP ...V...]]]]
 b. [AgrP ne+V+Agr [NegP pas [Neg t [VP ...t...]]]]

A theoretical question arises as to how the surface structure in (36b) is derived from (36a). Pollock proposes that *ne* is a syntactic clitic which left-adjoins to the Agr head, and that the verb moves to the same Agr head at the end of the derivation.[3] Assuming that clitic movement is an instance of left adjunction in French, the derivation of French negatives, as given in (36), is now illustrated in (37).

(37) a. [IP [NegP pas [Neg ne [VP ...V...]]]]
 Selected Substitution (V-to-I movement)
 b. [IP V+Agr [NegP pas [Neg ne [VP ...t ...]]]]
 Adjunction of *ne* to Infl [4]
 c. [IP ne+V+Agr [NegP pas [Neg t [VP ...t ...]]]]

In (37b, c), V raises and left-adjoins to Infl, via the intermediate Neg, and subsequently *ne* left-adjoins to the complex [V+Agr]. Given that the HMC is subsumed under the MLC, crossing an intermediate Neg is allowed since Neg-features are non-L-related, (cf. Chomsky 1989) and cannot be selected by V-related functional heads.

Wilder and Cavar (1994) show that Croatian exhibits a wide range of

---

[3] This head-to-head movement apparently violates the HMC, although the output representation may not do so. The solution he proposed is to reduce the HMC to the ECP, following Chomsky (1989). That is, an HMC violation is nullified if the LF representation does not violate the ECP (see also Belletti 1994).

[4] The structure in (37c) may violate the strict cycle condition. I assume, however, that the strict cycle does not apply to adjunction (cf. Chomsky 1993).

syntactic cliticization to a complementizer:

(38)   ...da me je Ivan vidio.
          that me be-3sg Ivan see-ptc
          '... that Ivan has seen me'

They claim that *me* and *je* in (38) are clitics, and that this clitic cluster is right adjoined to the complementizer *da*. Hence, no argument may separate the clitic cluster from the complementizer.

(39)   ...*da Ivan me je vidio.
          that Ivan me be-3sg see-ptc.

Sentence (39) shows that the subject cannot intervene between the complementizer and the clitic cluster *me je*. The subject can, however, intervene between the complementizer and a non-clitic finite verb, as illustrated in (40).

(40)   ...da Ivan nije vidio Damira.
          that Ivan Neg-be-3sg see-ptc Damira
          '...that Ivan didn't see Damir.'

Wilder and Cavar take the contrast between (39) and (40) as evidence suggesting that the clitic cluster *me je* right-adjoins to Comp. Furthermore, they show that in interrogative sentences in Croatian, the Q-particle right-adjoins to the complementizer as in (41).

(41)   ...da li ga Ivan vidi?
          that Q him Ivan see-3sg
          'Does Ivan see him?'

The cluster comprising the question morpheme and the object clitic is supported by the complementizer. Hence, if Comp is empty, the clitic cannot move.

(42) *Ga nije vidio.
him Neg-be-3sg see-ptc

I assume that the ungrammaticality of (42) is due to the Stranded Affix Filter condition, as given in (34). In the following, I will consider the behavior of Q-particles in Japanese and Sinhala, suggesting that Q-particles are treated as clitics.

In Sinhala, the Q-particle *də* directly marks *wh*-words and an E ending appears on the predicate as opposed to the A ending normally affixed to finite main verbs (cf. Sumangala 1992).[5] This is illustrated in the following examples:

(43) a. Siri waduwædə keruwA.
Siri woodworking do-Past-A
'Siri did woodworking.'
b. Siri mokak-də keruwE?
Siri what-Q did-E
'What did Siri do?'

Sinhala cannot have the Q-particle in clause-final position in matrix clauses, as shown in (44). When a *wh*-word is embedded in the complement clause of verbs like *dannəwa* 'know', and *æhuwa* 'ask', the Q-particle *də* may show up either in argument position or in clause-final position, as illustrated in (45a, b)

(44) *Kauru potə gatta-də?
who book bought-Q
'Who bought a book?'

---

[5] In Sinhala, non-interrogative focus elements have the same dependency relations.
(i) Bat-uy kankaave ayə kannE.
rice-Foc SiriLankans-Gen people eat-E
'It is rice that Sri Lankans eat.'
(ii) Citra-i potə kiewuwE.
Chitra-Foc book read
'It was Chitra that read the book.' (Sumangala 1992)

(45) a. Chitra [kau-də potə gatte kiyəla] dannəwa.
Chitra who-Q book bought that know
'Chitra knows who bought the book.'
b. Chitra [kauru potə gatta-də kiyəla] dannəwa.
Chitra who book bought-Q that know
'Chitra knows who bought the book.'

The difference in grammaticality between (44) and (45b) in Sinhara appears to be parallel to that between (46a) and (46b) in Japanese.

(46) a. *Dare-ga hon-o katta-ka?
who-Nom book-Acc bought-Q
'Who bought a book?'
b. [Dare-ga hon-katta-ka to] omotta.
who-Nom book bought-Q that thought.
'I wonder who bought a book.'

The contrast between (44) and (45b) in Sinhala and between (46a) and (46b) in Japanese suggests that the Q-particle behaves like a clitic. (44) and (46a) are not acceptable because a Q-particle, as a clitic, cannot move to an empty Comp due to the Stranded Affix Filter given in (34). In (45b) and (46b), on the other hand, the complementizer supports the cliticization of *də* and *ka*, yielding grammatical sentences. (For a detailed account of *ka*-movement, see section 3.4.)

3.3.3 I-to-C Movement in English

Turning to English, there is no such overt clitic. But I propose that I-to-C movement is driven by a covert Q base-adjoined to Foc.[6] I-to-C movement in English occurs not only in interrogatives but also when a negative constituent is fronted.

---

[6] Q refers to the operator features realized either overtly or covertly depending on the language.

(47) a. With no job John would be happy.
    b. With no job would John be happy.

Although the negative inversion in (47b) is not obligatory in English, (47a) and (47b) have different meanings. In (47b) the negative has scope over the entire clause, which corresponds to (48):

(48) John wouldn't be happy (with any job).

By contrast, (47a) has constituent scope; negation does not negate the entire clause but it only negates the property of 'having a job'. This means that the position of the negative phrase in the specifier of CP licenses clausal scope through a Spec-head agreement, while adjunction does not enter into the agreement relation and hence cannot have clausal scope. Clausal negation is only possible with non-interrogative sentences. Thus, consider (49).

(49) With no job, why would John be happy?

(49) is unambiguous in that it is interpreted only as constituent negation. Negation cannot have clausal scope in this case. This is straightforwardly accounted for, if clausal negation is possible only under a Spec-head agreement within CP. The negative inversion in (47b) conveys a focus reading, since Q is instantiated in Foc. Infl is morphologically realized by the auxiliary verb, and Q is excorporated from Foc and adjoined to Infl. The entire complex moves to Comp, as illustrated in (50).

(50)
```
            CP
          /    \
       Spec    C'
              /   \
         [Q+I]ᵢ+C  IP
                  /  \
                Spec  I'
                /    /  \
               tᵢ   FocP
                   /    \
                 Spec   Foc'
                       /    \
                     t+F    VP
```

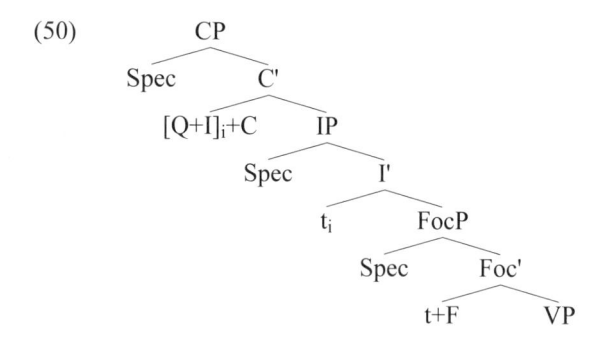

I-to-C movement is never found in indirect questions, while it is possible in embedded clauses selected by a bridge verb.

(51) a. He said that under no circumstances would he do it.
 b. *I wonder if/whether under no circumstances would John do that.

Assuming with Rizzi and Roberts (1989) that the complementizer *that* has the property of selecting another CP, in (51a) Q is adjoined to Foc and I-to-C movement takes place as a result of Q-movement. In (51b), Q originates in Comp and hence no I-to-C movement is possible.

3.3.4 Subject-Object Asymmetry

I assume that *wh*-questions involve two kinds of features [+Wh] and [+Q] (cf. Chomsky 1995). The *wh*-feature of Foc is weak and the Q-feature of Foc is universally strong. That is, in all languages the Q-feature is checked against Comp in the overt syntax. Now let us turn to Rizzi's (1991) *Wh*-Criterion given in (11), repeated below.

(52) The *Wh*-Criterion (Rizzi 1991)
 a. A *wh*-operator must be in a Spec-head configuration with an X^0 [+Wh].
 b. An X^0 [+Wh] must be in a Spec-head configuration with a *wh*-operator.

(52) states that at some level of derivation, a *wh*-operator must be in the

specifier position and [+Wh] in its head position. Given that there is a clause internal FocP, a possible structural position where [+Wh] stands in a Spec-head relation is FocP, IP or CP.

Let us now consider sentences (53a) and (53b).

(53) a. Who bought a book?
 b. What did Peter buy?

In the spirit of the analysis proposed above, checking of [+Wh] in (53a, b) takes place in different positions. This is illustrated in (54a, b).

(54) *Wh*-checking
 a. Who bought a book?
    [$_{IP}$ who Foc$_{wh}$+I [$_{FocP}$ t [$_{VP}$ buy a book]]]
 b. What did Peter buy?
    [$_{IP}$ Peter [$_{FocP}$ what$_i$ Foc$_{wh}$ [$_{VP}$ buy t$_i$]]]

In my account, Q/*wh*-features are the properties of Foc. Furthermore, *wh*-movement is derived by a strong Q-feature and a *wh*-feature is taken to be a "free rider." In (54a) Foc raises to Infl and this complex head stands in a Spec-head relation with the *wh*-phrase in the subject position. I assume that the *wh*-phrase in the subject position may not move to Spec(FocP) since movement from Spec(FocP) to Spec(IP) would create an improper chain. In other words, in sentence (54a), the *wh*-feature is checked as a free rider within the IP. In contrast, the *wh*-word in the object position in (54b) raises to Spec(FocP) and under this Spec-head relation, the *wh*-feature is checked off. Note that in both cases, Q-features must raise to Comp. In the case of the subject, Foc^0 moves to Infl and checks off the *wh*-feature. The entire complex [Foc+I] raises to Comp to check a strong Q. This is shown below:

(55) Q-checking
Who bought a book?
[$_{CP}$ who$_i$ [Foc+I]+C [$_{IP}$ t$_i$ [$_{FocP}$ t [$_{VP}$ bought a book]]]]

In the case of the object, Foc^0 may not move to Infl since the object does not agree in case-features with the subject. This is due to the following condition (Lasnik and Saito 1992).

(56) The Spec and head of a projection must agree in features at all points in the derivation prior to (and including) LF.

Although Foc^0 may not move, the Q in F moves to Comp in the overt syntax. In my analysis, Q is base-adjoined to Foc, as illustrated in (57).

(57)   Foc^0
           /   \
          Q   Foc^0

Following Roberts's (1991) analysis, as discussed earlier, excorporation of Q from Foc is possible since Q-movement is an instance of adjunction rather than substitution. *Do*-support is then instantiated as a last resort to provide a landing site for a clitic Q in accordance with condition (34), repeated below:

(58) Stranded Affix Filter
An affix must be a syntactic dependent of a morphologically realized category at surface structure.

Under my account, (58) is taken as a condition on clitic Q-movement and applies to both overt and covert Q. Given that *do*-support is required in the case of *wh*-movement of the object, (53b) has the derivation given in (59).

(59) What did Peter buy?
[$_{CP}$ what$_j$ [Q$_k$+did]$_i$+C [$_{IP}$ Peter t$_i$ [$_{FocP}$ t$_j$ [t$_k$+Foc] [$_{VP}$ buy t$_j$]]]]

The *wh*-object first moves to Spec(FocP) and subsequently moves to Spec(CP). Q is excorporated from Foc and adjoins to Infl, which is morphologically supported by *do*. The whole complex then moves to Comp to check a strong Q.

In English, the *wh*-feature of the subject is checked in the domain of IP since the subject necessarily moves to Spec(IP). In some languages an overt expletive element appears in Spec(IP) when the subject NP is focused and moves to Spec(FocP). For example, Horvath (1986) shows that in Aghem, all focused phrases and *wh*-phrases move to the postverbal focus position. When the subject appears in this position, the expletive *à* obligatorily appears in Spec(IP). This is illustrated in the following examples, taken from Horvath (1986).[7]

(60) a. éná? mɔ̀ ñ íŋ nô.
    Inah run Foc
    'Inah ran.'
  b. à mɔ̀ ñíŋ éná?
    Exp ran Inah
    'INAH ran.'
  c. à mɔ̀ ñíŋ ndúghɔ́?
    Exp ran who
    'Who ran?'

The structure of the sentences given in (60) is similar to the existential subject construction, shown in (61).

(61) There is a man in the garden.

---

[7] This postverbal focus position appears immediately adjacent to the verb, because when there are more than two elements, focus/*wh*-phrases must precede all other elements, as illustrated in (i).
  (i) fíl á mɔ́ zí zín bé-'kɔ́?
    friends SM P$_2$ eat when fufu
    'When did the friends eat fufu?'

There are a number of analyses concerning the Case assignment of the subject in the existential construction (cf. Chomsky 1986b). Although the issue is a matter of controversy, it is possible that subject Case is assigned in Aghem, similarly to the way subject Case is assigned in an existential construction in English.

3.3.5 *That*-Trace Effects

In the previous section, I illustrated Rizzi's ECP analysis of the contrast between the (a) and (b) examples of (62) and (63).

(62) a. Who left early?
b. *Who did leave early?

(63) a. Who do you think left early?
b. *Who do you think that t left early?

There have been many other attempts to account for *that*-trace effects within the theory of the ECP. Lasnik and Saito (1986, 1992) adopt a disjunctive formulation of the ECP to account for the subject-object asymmetry in English. The disjunctive formulation of the ECP predicts that an object trace is lexically governed, and hence *that*-trace effects never arise. Neither a subject nor an adjunct trace is lexically governed, so they must be antecedent-governed. According to Lasnik and Saito, a proper antecedent governor for a subject trace is not an intermediate trace left in Spec(CP) but is Comp, which is assigned the index of a *wh*-word through a Spec-head agreement. Lasnik and Saito (1992:179) propose the following condition:

(64) The index of Spec is copied onto the head only if the Spec and the head agree with respect to the feature [±Wh].

A Comp and a trace are unmarked for the features [±Wh]. In contrast, the complementizer *that* is intrinsically marked for [-Wh].

(65) a. Who do you think [t′ C [t left early]]?
b. *Who do you think [t′ that [t left early]]?

The intermediate trace t′ and the empty Comp in (65a) both lack the [+Wh] feature. Thus, this Comp is coindexed with its specifier and antecedent-governs the subject trace. In (65b), the intermediate trace t′ lacks the [+Wh] feature, but the overt complementizer *that* is [−Wh]. Since coindexation is not possible, the subject trace is not properly governed.

My proposed analysis will provide an account for *that*-trace effects without recourse to the ECP. I assume that Q as a clitic is an optional element in Foc, and that in (63), Q appears only in the matrix Foc. The *wh*-feature of Foc may appear in embedded Foc, but since this feature is weak and checked off as a free rider, no I-to-C movement is observed in the embedded clause. Given that Foc moves to Infl and that the *wh*-feature of the subject is checked within IP, the ungrammaticality of (63b) comes from the idiosyncratic properties of the complementizer *that*. Note that a complementizer has its own categorial feature specified as [±Wh] to indicate whether it is interrogative. At the same time, a complementizer has a selectional feature [±Finite] so that it can introduce a finite or non-finite clause. In other words, a complementizer must select a proper Infl that matches its own feature. If so, (63b) is not acceptable since *that* has a [-Wh] feature and cannot select Infl that has the conflicting [+Wh] feature.

Since English and German possess no morphologically realized Q, it is hard to see what is going on in *wh*-questions. In the following sections, I discuss the behavior of the Q-particle in Japanese. A number of pieces of empirical evidence suggest that the Q-particle is a morphological realization of a Q-feature, and that it is treated as a clitic that originates in Foc and moves to Comp.

3.4 Clitic Q-Movement in Japanese

3.4.1 Two Types of Verbals

Japanese has two forms of verbal expressions. One consists of a verb stem plus a tense affix; namely, one of the morphological affixes, *ta* (past tense) or *u* (present tense) is incorporated into a verb stem. The other form consists of a verb stem ending in a vowel (either *i* or *e*) with the auxiliary verb *masu* attached to it. *Masu* is an auxiliary verbal element which signals discoursal politeness. For expository purposes, we call the former inflected V forms, and the latter *masu*-forms. Japanese exhibits a matrix-embedded asymmetry with respect to these two types of forms. Inflected V forms are used in both matrix and embedded clauses, while *masu*-forms are used only in matrix clauses.[8]

(66) a. John-ga hon-o katta.
John-Nom book-Acc bought
'John bought a book.'
b. John-ga hon-o katta-to omotta.
John-Nom book-Acc bought-that thought
'I thought that John bought a book.'

(67) a. John-ga hon-o kai-masita.
John-Nom book-Acc buy-Aux
'John bought a book.'

---

[8] It is pointed out in the literature that *masu*-forms are possible inside an adverbial clause headed by *node*, 'because', but when these forms appear inside a clause headed by *node*, *node* may be taken as a conjunct. An example is given below.
  (i) John-ga ki-masita-node kaeri-masu.
  John-Nom come-Aux-Past because return-Aux
  'John came, (and) so I will go home.'
  (i.e., 'Because John came, I will go home.')

b. *John-ga hon-o kai-masita-to omoi-masita.
John-Nom book-Acc buy-Aux-that think-Aux
'I thought that John bought a book.'

The contrast between (66b) and (67b) shows that *masu*-forms are in general not permissible inside the embedded clause. If *masu* appears in some projection inside the clause, it is hard to see why there is a contrast. Suppose instead that *masu* is an auxiliary verb that undergoes V-to-C movement. Then this would straightforwardly account for the complementary distribution between *masu* and the complementizer *to*. I take this view as the null hypothesis. Following Chomsky (1993), I assume that the verb is drawn from the lexicon fully inflected, and merely checks its features against phonologically contentless functional heads. Since the auxiliary verb *masu* is inflected in the same way as the verb, I take *masu* to be base-generated inside a VP. *Masu* raises to Comp, as illustrated in (68).

(68)   [CP [IP [VP V t_i] t_i] masu$_i$+I+C] (V-to-C movement)

This construction-specific I-to-C movement in Japanese is triggered by operator-like features (i.e., mood) associated with *masu* and a head Foc.

3.4.2 The Q-particle *Ka*

It is well known that *wh*-questions in Japanese take three different forms. Interrogatives are either marked by a question particle *ka* (*ka*-interrogatives), or by the complementizer *no* (*no*-interrogatives). Interrogatives can also be morphologically unmarked (ϕ-interrogatives).[9] Some complications arise with respect to these three types of *wh*-questions. *Ka*-interrogatives are possible with *masu*-forms but not with inflected V-forms. In contrast, the situation for *no*-interrogatives is reversed; they are possible with inflected V-forms but not with

---

[9] Although ϕ-interrogatives contain no overt Q-particles, I assume that a phonologically unrealized null Q is associated with the interrogatives and moves to Comp.

masu-forms. ɸ-interrogatives, on the other hand, can be used with either *masu*-forms or inflected V-forms. This is illustrated in the following examples.

(69) *No*-interrogatives:
    a. Mary-ga nani-o yonda-no?
       Mary-Nom what-Acc read-C$_{[+Q]}$
       'What did Mary read?'
    b. *Mary-ga nani-o yomi-masita-no?
       Mary-Nom what-Acc read-Aux-C$_{[+Q]}$

(70) *Ka*-interrogatives:
    a. *Mary-ga nani-o yonda-ka?
       Mary-Nom what-Acc read-Q
       'What did Mary read?'
    b. Mary-ga nani-o yomi-masita-ka?
       Mary-Nom what-Acc read-Aux-Q

(71) ɸ-interrogatives:
    a. Mary-ga nani-o yonda?
       Mary-Nom what-Acc read
       'What did Mary read?'
    b. Mary-ga nani-o yomi-masita?
       Mary-Nom what-Acc read-Aux

The complementary distribution between the particle *no* and the auxiliary *masu* as shown in (69b) is accounted for straightforwardly by the assumption that *no* is a complementizer base-generated in Comp.[10] In other words, the *no*-interrogatives in (69) are treated in the same way as interrogatives in languages

---

[10] *No*-interrogatives have syntactic and semantic properties different from *ka*-interrogatives. I will discuss the differences in Chapter 4 and argue that *no*-interrogatives are treated as reduced clefts, which contain a phonologically empty sequence of *desu-ka* (copula-Q).

like Kinande and Egyptian Arabic, where a *wh*-complementizer is base-generated in Comp, as shown in (72a) and (72b) respectively.

(72) a. IyondI y⁰ kambale alangIra?
   who that Kambale saw
   'Who did Kambale see?' (Rizzi 1990a)
   b. Miin illi Mona darabit-uh?
   who that Mona hit-him
   'Who did Mona hit?' (Wahba 1984)

Let us now turn to *ka*-interrogatives which do not appear with inflected V-forms. Example (70a) may have the following derivation.

(73) *Mary-ga nani-o yonda-ka?
   a. [FocP [VP...yonda] Foc+ka] (Base Structure)
   b. * [[FocP [VP...yonda] Foc+tᵢ] kaᵢ] (Excorporation of Q to Infl)

As discussed previously, *ka* is a clitic that must satisfy the general property associated with clitic movement; that is, a clitic ends up in a position that provides morphological support. In (73), the clitic moves to the empty head, which leads to a violation of the Stranded Affix Filter in (34).

In (70b), on the other hand, *masu* provides morphological support and the entire complex moves to Comp. The derivation of (70b) is represented in (74).

(74) Mary-ga nani-o yomi masita-ka?
   [CP [IP [FocP [VP...yomi t] t] t] [masita+ka]+C]

(74) involves successive cyclic V-to-C movement and the entire complex left-adjoined to Comp. The head movement to Comp is driven by the Q-feature in the same way as in *wh*-questions in English and V2 languages suggested earlier. In the following section, I will present supporting evidence for the view that *ka*

moves from Foc to Comp.

3.4.3 Embedded *Wh*-Questions

This section discusses embedded *wh*-questions which are selected by the Q-particle *ka*, and those selected by the complementizer *to* 'that'. It is argued that *ka* is directly generable in Comp only in the context where Q is assigned by a higher verb having the property of selecting a [+Q] Comp. There are three types of verbs which select embedded *wh*-questions. Verbs such as *siru* 'know' and *oboeru* 'remember' select a [+Q] Comp and do not allow the complementizer *to* to mark embedded questions. On the other hand, verbs such as *omou* 'think' select *wh*-questions obligatorily marked by *to*. Finally, verbs like *tazuneru* 'ask' can take two types of clauses: clauses marked by *ka* and those by *to*. This is illustrated in the following examples.

(75) a. Mary-ga nani-o yonda-ka sira-nai.
    Mary-Nom what-Acc read-Q know-not
    'I don't know what Mary read.'
  b. *Mary-ga nani-o yonda-ka-to sira-nai.
    Mary-Nom what-Acc read-Q-that know-not

(76) a. Mary-ga nani-o yonda-ka-to omotta.
    Mary-Nom what-Acc read-Q-that thought
    'I wonder what Mary read.'
  b. *Mary-ga nani-o yonda-ka omotta.
    Mary-Nom what-Acc read-Q thought

(77) a. Mary-ga nani-o yonda-ka-to tazuneta.
    Mary-Nom what-Acc read-Q-that asked
    'I asked what Mary read.'
  b. Mary-ga nani-o yonda-ka tazuneta.
    Mary-Nom what-Acc read-Q asked

The complementizer *to* is not allowed in (75), while it is obligatory in (76). In (77), *to* is optional. These three types of verbs have different syntactic properties, which are illustrated below.

3.4.3.1 Focus Particles and Question Particles

It has been shown in Chapter 2 that focus particles cannot co-occur with question particles in the root clause, as shown in (78).

(78) *Kimi-wa [FocP [VP nani-o kai]-wa/sae] si-masita-ka?
　　　you-Top　　　　what-Acc buy-Foc do-Aux-Q
　　　'What did you even buy?'

In (78), the focus particle and the question particle are licensed in Foc and hence they are in complementary distribution. However, there is a difference within embedded *wh*-questions, as illustrated below.

(79) a. ?[Mary-ga nani-o kai-wa/sae sita-ka] sira-nai.
　　　　Mary-Nom what-Acc buy-Foc did-Q know-not
　　　　'I don't know what Mary bought even.'
　　b. *[Mary-ga nani-o kai-wa/sae sita-ka-to] omotta.
　　　　Mary-Nom what-Acc buy-Foc did-Q-that thought
　　　　'I wonder what Mary bought even.'
　　c. *[Mary-ga nani-o kai-wa/sae sita-ka-(to)] tazuneta.
　　　　Mary-Nom what-Acc buy-Foc did-Q-that asked
　　　　'I asked what Mary bought even.'

Although sentence (79a) is not perfect, it is significantly better than sentences (79b) and (79c).[11] The grammaticality status of (79b) and (79c) is the same as that of (78). (79a) is acceptable because the matrix verb selects [+Q] Comp and *ka* originates in Comp, not in Foc. In contrast, the matrix verb in (79b, c)

---

[11] For some native Japanese speakers, sentence (79a) is completely acceptable.

selects [-Q] Comp and *ka* undergoes clitic Q-movement in the same way as in root clauses. Consider (76a, b), repeated in (80a, b).

(80) a. [Mary-ga nani-o yonda-ka-to] omotta.
Mary-Nom what-Acc read-Q-that thought
'I wonder what Mary read.'
b. *[Mary-ga nani-o yonda-ka] omotta.
Mary-Nom what-Acc read-Q thought

The verb *omou* selects the [-Q] complementizer *to* and thus (80a) involves clitic Q-movement, as represented in (81)

(81) [$_{CP}$ [$_{IP}$ [$_{FocP}$ [$_{VP}$ ...yonda] t+Foc] I] ka-to] omotta

In (81) the clitic *ka* is moved from Foc and left-adjoined to the complementizer *to*. Recall that excoporation of *ka* to an empty head is not possible because it leads to a violation of the Stranded Affix Filter in (34). While in (80a) the complementizer *to* provides morphological support for the clitic *ka*, in (80b) movement of the clitic *ka* is ruled out by this condition.

3.4.3.2 The Copula *Da* and *Desu* in Japanese

This section shows that two types of copula provide another piece of evidence supporting the view that embedded *wh*-questions selected by the complementizer *to* 'that' involve clitic Q-movement. Adjectivals and nominals take the copula form *desu* or *da*. These two types of copula behave exactly parallel to *masu* forms and inflected V forms respectively. Namely, the copula *desu* cannot be used inside embedded clauses, while *da* can be used in both root and embedded clauses.[12] This is illustrated in (82).

---

[12] The observation concerning the copula *da* originally comes from Ueyama (1992).

(82) a. Gakusei desu/da.
        student be
      b. [Gakusei *desu/da-to] omoi-masu.
        student   be   that think-Aux
        '(I) think (he) is a student.'
      c. [Dare *desu/da-ka] siri-mas-en.
        who   be-Q   know-Aux-not
        '(I) don't know who (he) is.'

The copula *da* can be analyzed as the amalgamation of the copula V and the present tense. *Desu*, on the other hand, constitutes the copula stem *de* and the inflected auxiliary *si* 'do'. Let us hypothesize that the copula *da* and *desu*-forms have the following structures.

(83) a. [IP [VP ...da]]
      b. [CP [IP [VP ...de t] t] su]   (V-to-C movement)

While the copula stem stays *in-situ*, the auxiliary *su* raises to Comp, which is driven by mood features associated with the auxiliary verb. (I assume that 'clause-type' or 'Mood' is a property of Foc.) Now consider (84a, b).

(84) a. *John-wa [VP dare da] ka?
        John-Top   who be Q
        'Who is John?'
      b. John-wa [VP dare de] su-ka?
        John-Top   who be Aux-Q
        'Who is John?'

(84a) is not acceptable since *ka* as a clitic may not be adjoined to the empty Comp, as discussed above. In (84b), on the other hand, *su* provides morphological support for *ka*-movement.

Let us now turn to embedded questions with the copula *da*. The sequence of *da* and the Q-particle *ka* is permitted only in a context in which the verb selects a [+Q] Comp. Verbs such as *wakaru* 'understand' select a [+Q] Comp and the sequence *da-ka* is possible, as illustrated in (85).

(85) [John-ga dare da-ka] wakara-nai.
      John-Nom who be-Q know-not
      'I don't know who John is.'

I have suggested that *ka* is base-generated in [+Q] Comp selected by verbs such as *wakaru* 'understand' and hence (85) involves no clitic Q-movement. Now consider the complement of verbs, such as *tazuneru* 'ask', which select the complementizer *to*. Compare the contrast given in (86a, b).

(86) a. *Kanozyo-wa [John-ga dare da ka-to] tazuneta.
          she-Top   John-Nom who be Q-that ask
          'She asked who John is.'
      b. Kanozyo-wa [John-ga dare ka-to] tazuneta.
         she-Top   John-Nom who Q-that asked
         'She asked who John is.'

Sentences (86a) and (86b) differ only in that the former contains a *da-ka* sequence, as opposed to the latter, which contains no such sequence. The contrast in grammaticality shows that the *da-ka* sequence is not possible if the verb selects a CP headed by the complementizer *to*. Recall that under my analysis, *ka* in embedded clauses is adjoined to Comp. Thus, example (87) is derived by clitic Q-movement to the complementizer *to*.

(87) Kanozyo-wa [John-ga nani-o yonda ka-to] tazuneta.
      she-Top John-Nom what-Acc read Q-that ask
      'She asked what John read.'

A question that arises is why the same derivation is not possible in (86a). One way to account for the ungrammaticality of (86a) is to assume that the copula *da* in Japanese is inherently focused and it directly appears in Foc. (Awobuluyi (1992) made the similar claim that in Yoruba, the element *ni* has dual categorial status, as a copula verb and simultaneously as a focus particle.) Note that the copula *da* 'be' in Japanese is not semantically vacuous, but conveys the mood property [+Assertive]. While the copula *da* can appear inside a complement clause selected by *to* as in (88a), it fails to appear inside a factive complement selected by *koto* 'fact', as in (88b).

(88) a. Boku-wa [John-ga isha da-to] omotta.
     I-Top John-Nom doctor be-that thought
     'I thought that John was a doctor.'
   b. *Boku-wa [John-ga isha da koto-o] sitteiru.
     I-Top John-Nom doctor be that-Acc know
     'I know (the fact) that John is a doctor.'

If *da* were simply a copula verb, we would have no account for the contrast given in (88a, b). Note that focused phrases may not appear inside factive complements selected by *koto* 'fact', as illustrated in (89).

(89) a. *Kimi-wa [John-ga naze kita koto-o] oboeteiru-no?
     you-Top John-Nom why came that-Acc remember-Q
     'Why$_i$ do you remember that John came t$_i$?'
   b. *Kimi-wa [John-ga ittai nani-o nonda koto-o] oboeteiru-no?
     you-Top John-Nom OP what-Acc drank that-Acc remember-Q
     'What do you remember that John drank t?'
   c. *Boku-wa [John-ga hon-sae katta koto-o] oboeteiru.
     I-Top John-Nom book-even bought that-Acc remember
     'I remember that John bought even books.'

The fact that focused phrases do not occur inside *koto* 'fact'-clauses suggests that mood or clause-type features such as [+Factive] and [+Assertive] are properties of Foc and hence they are in complementary distribution with focus elements. This in turn supports the view that the copula *da* having the property of [+Assertive] is an element of Foc. Given that FocP cannot be headed by multiple heads, the *da-ka* sequence is impossible in sentences like (86a), where *ka* originates in Foc. (85), on the other hand, is acceptable since *ka* directly appears in Comp and involves no clitic Q-movement.

The next section will further examine the asymmetry between the two types of complement clauses, and present cross-linguistic evidence that operator features are base-generable in [+Q] Comp, while they are generated in the clause-internal Foc when the complementizer has a [-Q] Comp.

3.4.4 Cross-Linguistic Evidence

Rizzi and Roberts (1989) suggest that negative inversion is an instance of I-to-C movement. I-to-C movement is never found in indirect questions, while it is possible in the complement of bridge verbs.

(90) a. He said that under no circumstances would he do it.

b. *I wonder if/whether under no circumstances would John do that.

Rizzi and Roberts argue that CP recursion is possible only in (90a) with [-Wh] Comp. Suppose that negative inversion is triggered by clitic Q-movement, as discussed above. Then, examples (90a, b) show that the complement of a bridge verb involves movement, while the complement of a verb selecting a [+Q] Comp involves no movement. The difference between the two types of verbs has also been pointed out by Laka (1990), who shows that negative polarity items (NPIs) are licensed only inside the complement of negative verbs, such as *deny*, *regret* and *forget*.

(91) a. The witness denied [that anybody left the room before dinner].

b. The professor doubts [that anybody understood her explanation].

These verbs, however, do not license NPIs in their object position:

(92) a. *The witnesses denied anything.
    b. *The professor doubts any explanation.

This means that a Comp selected by those negative verbs is the licenser for NPIs. NPIs are, however, never licensed by a Comp selected by the bridge verb.

(93) *The witness said that anybody left the room before dinner.

Laka concludes that the complementizer of a negative verb is specified as that$_{NEG}$, which licenses NPIs. On the other hand, the complementizer of bridge verbs cannot be endowed with the feature [+Neg], and hence licensing of NPIs is impossible. This is consistent with my view that the operator feature Q is directly base-generable in Comp, only if it is selected by a higher verb.

Finally, German provides further evidence for the asymmetry between the two types of verbs. Recall that in German, verb movement never occurs in embedded questions, as shown in (94). (German examples are cited from Vikner 1990.)

(94) a. Ich weiß nicht, welchen film die Kinder gesehen haben.
         I   know not   which   film the children have   seen

    b. *Ich weiß nicht, welchen film haben die Kinder gesehen.
        I   know not   which   film have   the children seen

In (94a, b), the embedded Comp contains the feature [+Q]. The ungrammaticality of (94b) indicates that when [+Q] features are generated in Comp, no verb movement is possible. In German, if the Comp selected by the bridge verb contains no lexical complementizer, V2 is obligatory, as illustrated in the following examples.

(95) a. *Johann glaubt, er Maria liebt immer noch.
        John   thinks he Mary loves still

b. Johann glaubt, er liebt Maria immer noch.
John thinks he loves Mary still

(96) a. *Er sagt, die Kinder diesen Film gesehen haben.
He says the children this film seen have
b. Er sagt, die Kinder haben diesen Film gesehen.
He says the children have this film seen

The fact that the complement of the verb selecting the [-Q] Comp exhibits head movement lends support to the view that operator features are generated inside the clause.

3.5 Summary

In this chapter, I have argued that Q in an unselected context originates in Foc and involves clitic Q-movement, while Q in a selected context is directly base-generated in Comp. While the clitic Q is morphologically realized as *ka* in Japanese, languages that possess no overt Q may have a covert Q (i.e., a null clitic). *Do*-support in English, for example, is seen as a last resort operation to host a null clitic Q. The Q-movement hypothesis proposed in this chapter gives a principled account for a wide range of construction-specific phenomena, such as V2 effects in Germanic languages, *that*-trace effects, presence or absence of I-to-C movement, and finally, asymmetries between subjects and objects and between root and embedded questions in various languages including Japanese.

4

Case/Focus Particles and Clause Structure Change: Evidence From Early Old Japanese

4.1 Introduction

Since Lightfoot's (1979) generative approach to syntactic change, the term "reanalysis" has received much attention in the literature. Reanalysis has been referred to as categorial change of an element, which often gives rise to overall clause structure change of a given language (cf. Whitman 2000, Roberts and Roussou 2003). Under a minimalist approach to diachronic syntax, Roberts and Roussou (2003) argue that a categorial change of a head always involves gain or loss of movement. In this chapter, I show that Japanese underwent clause structure change that is described by gain or loss of movement and that a categorial change of *ga* and so-called *kakari*-particles is directly responsible for this change.

In the previous chapters, I assume that subjects in Modern Japanese move to Spec(TP) (cf. Takezawa 1987), and argued that focus projection appears in a clause internal position between the subject and the VP in Japanese. In this chapter, I argue that in early Old Japanese (henceforth OJ), subjects with the case particle *ga* must stay *in-situ*, and that movement of the subject is a historical innovation caused by reanalysis of *ga*. *No*-marked subjects differ crucially from *ga*-marked subjects in that they can move to the sentence initial topic position. Furthermore, OJ has two types of objects. I show that while bare objects stay *in-situ*, objects with the particle *wo* must appear in a particular structural position outside a VP. In order to provide a principled account for the correlation between these particles and clause structure change, I propose that some particles, which are assumed to be postpositions, are in fact clausal heads that select VP complements on their right. The view that Japanese clauses are headed by the nominative case *ga* or the topic marker *wa* was originally suggested in Kayne (1994:143) in light of the Linear Correspondence Axiom (LCA) (see also Whitman 2001).[1] Given that the particle *ga* is a clausal head selecting a VP as its complement, my investigation discovered that *ga*-marked clauses underwent syntactic change, not internal to Japanese syntax, but comparable with *to*-infinitives in English.

Before providing extensive discussion concerning the clause structure of OJ, I will first discuss reanalysis of *to*-infinitives in English, showing that a structural change of infinitival clauses is caused by a change in the categorial feature of *to*.

4.2 Reanalysis

4.2.1 To-Infinitives

Under a minimalist approach to diachronic syntax, Roberts and Roussou (2003) suggest that reanalysis reduces to a change in the abstract features of functional heads. *To*-infinitives in English arguably underwent reanalysis of purposive adjuncts to complement clauses, as illustrated in (1) (cf. Lightfoot 1979, Los 1999, Fischer et al. 2000, Miller 2002, Roberts and Roussou 2003, and others).

---

[1] The LCA predicts that head-complement order (H-C) reflects universal order while complement-head order (C-H) is derived from movement of a complement over a head. From a number of empirical considerations, I assume that while functional categories are invariably head-initial, basic word order inside lexical projections is strictly head-final in Japanese. (For its theoretical implications, see section 4.6.)

(1) [VP [VP ...V] PP] > [VP V CP]

The [*for* NP *to* V] construction also results from reanalysis of a matrix PP as the subject of a subordinate clause, as represented in (2)

(2) V [PP for NP_i] [IP PRO_i to VP] > V [CP for [IP NP to VP]]

Roberts and Roussou (2003) argue that the reanalysis of an adjunct as a complement shown in (1) and (2) involves categorial reanalysis of *to* and *for*, which gives rise to so-called 'structural simplification'; that is, complements are structurally simpler than adjuncts in X' theoretic terms. Note, however, that the structural change illustrated in (2) does not reflect the fact that [*for* NP *to* V] constructions emerged without the NP (i.e., *forto* V). The *forto*-infinitives were used in the same context as *to*-infinitives, as exemplified by (3).

(3) hwet is mare medschipe flen [forto leuen on him...]
'What is more madness than to believe in him...'
(Idem, 325-7: Gelderen 1993, 87)

Whitman (2000) argues that a change caused by the categorial reanalysis of a head involves no structural modification of the sort proposed in (1) and (2), but that this class of reanalysis, which he calls "relabeling," involves only a simple change in the categorial feature of *for*, *to* and infinitival verbs, as described in (4).

(4) Relabeling (Whitman 2000:223)
The first step of syntactic analysis is restricted to relabeling, where relabeling refers to a change in the categorial feature of a head. The result of relabeling must be well-formed independently of any changes outside the minimal domain of the relabeled items.

Adopting the definition of "minimal domain" given in Chomsky (1995:178),

Whitman (2000) argues that a categorial change of a head generally triggers other changes that are limited to the "minimal domain" of that head including the specifier and the complement of that head. The view that *to*-infinitives underwent the structural change given in (1) and (2) is inconsistent with (4). The minimal domain of *for* includes only the NP c-commanded by *for*, and hence a categorial change of *for* may not affect *to*-infinitives.

It is widely assumed that the *to* in *to*-infinitives in Old English (OE) is a preposition. As a preposition, it assigns dative Case to an infinitive verb, which points to the infinitive verb being nominal rather than verbal. In this view, *to*-infinitives have the form represented in (5).

(5) [$_{PP}$ to [V$_{[+N]}$ ...]]

An infinitive verb takes a dative inflectional morpheme *-ne*, and appears as a GOAL argument to an adjective or a verb of motion such as *come* and *go*, as illustrated in (6a, b) (though they are arguably purposive adjuncts).

(6) a. ne com ic [sybbe to sendanne].
     'I did not come to send peace.'
                    (First West Saxon Gospel: Miller 2002, 188)
    b. Heo bið æfre geare [men to acwellene].
     'She is always ready to kill men.'
                    (LS 29, 340, H&V:Kageyama 1992, 116)

If *to* is a preposition and infinitive verbs are nominals, a question arises as to how the object of infinitive verbs is ever assigned Case. Fischer (1994) speculates that an object receives oblique Case from infinitive verbs, which are nouns, but can assign Case in OE. Kemenade (1993), however, rejects the idea that *to*-infinitives are nouns. If *to*-infinitives have the structure in (5), it is not clear how to derive the word order [OBJ *to*-V], where the object precedes the *to*-infinitive verb. Given that OE is an OV language, Kemenade proposes that *to* is interpreted as a preposition in Infl, and that an infinitive verb is right-adjoined to Infl, resulting in [OBJ t$_i$ *to*-V$_i$] order. Kageyama (1992), however, rejects the view that *to* appears in Infl (or Tense) since it fails to account for differences between OE and Modern English. *To*-infinitives in OE do not allow perfective or progressive forms, which began to appear in Middle English. (Kageyama assumes that aspectual auxiliaries are licensed by Tense.) *To*-infinitives in OE do not take a lexical subject (cf. Lightfoot 1991, 81). They are negated not by *ne*, but by *na* or *no*, which applies to constituents other than finite verbs. According to Kageyama, these properties of *to*-infinitives in OE show that they do not project to TP. He instead proposes that *to* is a preposition in Agr, and that *to*-infinitives have the structure [$_{AgrP}$ to [$_{VP}$...]], where *to* has the [-V, -N] feature. In other words, *to* has dual categorial status, as a preposition and simultaneously as a functional category Agr. The view that *to* is in Agr, however, is problematic if we take into account Los's (1999) observations concerning distributional similarities between *to*-infinitives and subjunctive *that*-clauses. Los indicates that verbs which select subjunctive *that*-clauses also select *to*-infinitives in OE. She then argues that *to* underwent no categorial change, and that *to*-infinitives have the status of CP, having a covert complementizer. Under her analysis, *to*-infinitive clauses in OE have the following structure.

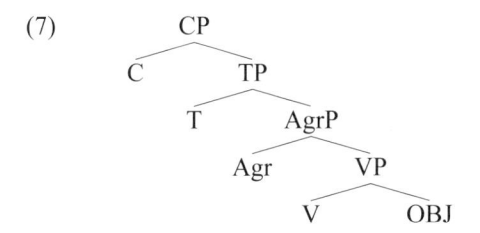

(7)
```
          CP
         /  \
        C    TP
            /  \
           T   AgrP
               /  \
             Agr   VP
                  /  \
                 V   OBJ
```

[OBJ to-V] order in OE is derived from overt movement of the object to Spec(AgrP). The clitic *to* is attached to the verb, but moves covertly to Comp successive cyclically through Tense. In other words, *to* has a tense feature to start with and *to*-infinitives involve no structural change. Los, however, provides no obvious empirical evidence for the existence of Tense except that it is the intermediate landing site for covert movement of the clitic *to*.

Gelderen (1993) follows the model of syntactic change developed by Lightfoot (1979, 1991) and argues that Tense should only be included in the structure of a language if there exists positive evidence, such as elements that exist in Tense in the overt syntax. While in modern English the existence of Tense is evidenced by a number of syntactic phenomena, OE lacks all the properties that indicate the existence of Tense. Namely, *there*-expletive constructions do not appear until the latter half of the fourteenth century. Modals were still main verbs. The first instance of *do*-support occurred in the late fourteenth century. The *to* in *to*-infinitives is treated as a clitic attached to an infinitive verb. Given that OE lacks elements that appear in Tense, Gelderen claims that OE simply lacks Tense and that the clause is either a VP, or a CP.[2] Now let us assume with Gelderen (1993) that OE lacks Tense, but that *to*-infinitives have the status of CP given the distributional evidence presented by Los (1999). That is, *to*-infinitive clauses have the structure in (8).

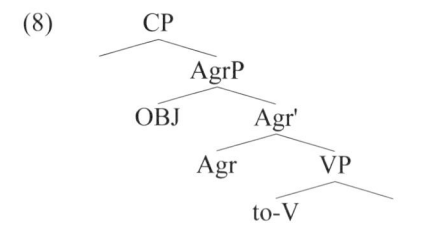

(8)
```
        CP
        |
       AgrP
       /  \
     OBJ   Agr'
           /  \
         Agr   VP
               |
              to-V
```

Note importantly that *to*-infinitives in OE rarely occur in the subject position (cf. Lightfoot 1979:201). Lightfoot observes that from the tenth to the fourteenth century the *to*-infinitive construction occurred as a 'logical subject' in the typical extraposed position. The following examples are cited from Miller (2002:198).

---

[2] The absence of the functional category Tense does not mean an absence of tense and agreement features. Tense and agreement can be seen as sets of features not necessarily connected with the head of TP. Gelderen (1993) proposes that in OE the tense and agreement features occupy a Comp.

(9) a. Now it is right [me to procede].   (RRose B3787: Miller 2002)
'Now it is right for me to proceed.'
b. It is inpossible [a sinner to gete...]   (Cloud 41/20f.fo.39a: Miller 2002)
'It is impossible for a sinner to get...'

Under the assumption that *to*-infinitives project to CP, the *to*-infinitives in (9a, b) are not extraposed, but rather they appear in the base position selected by the matrix adjective. Given that the adjectives in (9a, b) select a CP headed by the complementizer *that*, it is plausible that *to*-infinitives have the status of CP, as proposed by Los (1999).

It is widely known that *to*-infinitives underwent pervasive changes in Middle English (ME). The dative inflection started to disappear, and *forto* started to appear in late OE and spread rapidly in ME (cf. Gelderen 1993, Miller 2002). The dative subject in *to*-infinitives emerged in the forms of (i) to NP V, (ii) NP *to* V, and (iii) *for* NP *to* V. What is important for our purposes is that (*for*)*to*-infinitives emerged prior to the [for NP to V] construction, as indicated by Gelderen. If the subject of infinitives is the object of the matrix PP as in (2), we have no principled account for how the [for NP to V] construction evolved from *forto*-infinitives. In what follows, I assume with Whitman (2000) that reanalysis of (*for*)*to*-infinitives is viewed as a change in the categorial feature of *for* and *to*, which resulted in the emergence of the overt subject in *to*-infinitives. Given that *to*-infinitive clauses in OE have the structure (8), the structural change of *forto*-infinitives is represented in (10).

(10)   [$_{CP}$ [$_{VP}$ forto V]] > [$_{CP}$ for [$_{TP}$ to [$_{VP}$ V]]] > [$_{CP}$ for [$_{TP}$ SUBJ to [$_{VP}$ V]]]

In summary, reanalysis of (*for*)*to*-infinitives involves no modification of their surface structure, as illustrated in (2), but is a direct consequence of the categorical change of *for*, *to* and the infinitive verb that is "closely c-commanded" by *to*.

4.2.2 *Ga*-Marked Clauses

In Old Japanese (OJ), matrix clauses differ crucially from embedded clauses in that arguments tend to appear without a case particle and that caseless subjects take a predicate in the conclusive form. This is illustrated in (11).

(11) Nanifa-no miya-ni <u>wago ookimi</u> <u>kuni</u> sirasu-rasi (M. 933)
Naniwa-Gen court-Loc my emperor country govern-Aux-Con
'In the Naniwa Court, the emperor might govern the country.'

It is known that *ga*-marked subjects occur freely inside embedded clauses, but that when they appear in matrix clauses, they occur only with a predicate in the attributive form (cf. Sasaki 1996):

(12) a. [fito-mo naki munasiki ife-fa] ...kurusikari keri (M. 451)
man-also without vacant house-Top lonely-Past-Con
'My vacant house without any sign of man looked lonely.'
b. Siga sasare nami sikusiku-ni tuneni-to kimi-ga
Shiga ripple wave ceaselessly ever-as lord-Subj
omofoseri-keru (M. 206)
wish-for-Past-At
'As waves of Shiga rising on the rippling lake tap the sands ever and ceaselessly, the lord hoped (to live long).'

In (12a), the subject marked by the topic marker *wa* occurs with the auxiliary verb *keri* in the conclusive form, and in (12b) the subject marked by *ga* occurs with *keru* in the attributive form. The attributive predicate in OJ differs from that in Modern Japanese in that it has substantive interpretations. Thus, unlike Modern Japanese, the attributive predicate in OJ takes a case particle directly without the assistance of a pronominal genitive particle *no*. This is illustrated in (13a-c), cited from Motohashi (2003).

(13) a. [_S takubutsuma tsayagu]-ga sita-ni...
    cloth coverlet rustle-Subj   under
    'beneath the rustling of the cloth coverlet'   (Kojiki Kayoo 5)

b. [_S Yamato-he-ni yuku]-wa ta-ga   tuma
    Yamato-Loc   go-Top   who-Gen husband
    'Whose husband is that that is going to Yamato?'   (Kojiki Kayoo 56)

Furthermore, a clause with an attributive predicate can be the subject of a matrix clause, as in (14).

(14) [_S siratama-no kimi-ga yosofi-si] tafutoku ari keri.
      jowel-Gen you-Subj dress-up-Aux precious be-Past
      'Your appearance was precious like a white jewel.'   (Kojiki Kayoo 7)

It is widely observed among traditional grammarians that the merger of attributive and conclusive predicates is historically related to reanalysis of the genitive *ga* as a nominative *ga* (cf. Yanagida 1985, Ohno 1977, Yamada 2000). The reanalysis of *ga* not only leads to the merger of the two verbal forms, but also affects the type of predicates that it selects. Yamada (2000) examined the occurrence of *ga*, by comparing the Tale of *Heike*, which is believed to reflect the language of the fourteenth century with the later text of *Heike*, published in 1592 and known as *Amakusa Heike*.[3] As indicated in the following table, Yamada found 1600 examples of unmarked subjects in *Heike*, 290 of which were marked by *ga* in *Amakusa Heike*. (The subject NPs marked by other particles are not included.)

---

[3] *Amakusa Heike* contains many of the same stories as *Heike*. It was written as a textbook to teach Japanese to foreign missionaries.

(15) Unmarked vs. Marked Subjects in Amakusa Heike (Yamada 2000)

	Relative clause	Subordinate	Main	Complex	Total
Ga	36(20.2%)	152 (33%)	84 (27.5%)	18 (2.7%)	290 (18%)
No	42(23.6%)	10(2.25)	4(1.35)	1(0.2%)	57(3.6%)
unmarked	96(53.9%)	227(50%)	123(40.2%)	526(80.4%)	972(61.1%)

Despite the predominant use of unmarked subjects, the table reveals that the occurrence of *ga* significantly increased in *Amakusa Heike*. 27.5% of the subjects in the matrix clause came to be marked by *ga*. Yamada observes that although the matrix use of *ga* increased drastically in *Amakusa Heike*, the distribution of *ga* in this period differs significantly from that in modern Japanese. The following table shows the distribution of *ga* in main clauses, cited from Yamada (2000).

(16) *Ga* and Predicate Type in Main Clauses (Yamada 2000)

	Noun	transitive	unergative	adjective	unaccusative	Total
Ga	0(0%)	2(2%)	13 (16%)	15(18%)	54(64%)	84(100%)

In OJ, *ga* was used as a genitive particle modifying the following noun phrase, but the data reveals that nouns with *ga* had already disappeared by the time *Amakusa Heike* was written. Although the particle *ga* started to select verbal predicates, it was restricted to intransitive verbs, in particular, unaccusative verbs, and rarely occurred with transitive verbs.

To account for the change of *ga*-marked clauses discussed above, I suggest that *ga* is not a postposition, but rather a clausal head taking a VP as its complement (cf. Kayne 1994, Whitman 2001), as shown in (17).[4]

---

[4] Given that the structure of a noun phrase is parallel to that of a clause, I assume that the genitive particle is the head of a noun phrase. Whitman (2001) examines the structure of noun phrases in detail within Kayne's (1994) antisymmetry approach.

(17) [Subject NP [ga [VP....]]]

The idea that *ga* is a clausal head makes it possible to reduce change of *ga*-marked clauses to reanalysis of the particle *ga*. Change in the abstract feature of *ga* contributed to change that occurred inside the VP since the VP is in the 'minimal domain' of *ga*. It follows that change of *ga*-marked clauses, which has been analyzed as strictly internal to Japanese syntax, falls into the same general category of change as *to*-infinitives in English discussed in section 4.2.1.

4.3 The Position of Subjects

There is a long-standing debate concerning whether the subject in Japanese raises to Spec(TP) or appears inside a VP. A problem has to do with the fact that, contrary to English, Japanese has little positive evidence for functional categories outside a VP. This leads some researchers to believe that Japanese clauses do not project to TP and that the subject stays inside the VP (cf. Fukui 1986, Kuroda 1988). Takezawa (1987), however, provides evidence showing that nominative subjects are licensed by Tense. Consider the examples below:

(18) a. Taroo-wa [[Hanako-ga/o utsukusii] to] omotta.
       Taroo-Top Hanako-Nom/Acc beautiful that thought
       'Taroo thought that Hanako was beautiful.'
    b. Taroo-wa [Hanako-*ga/o utsukusi-ku] omotta.
       Taroo-Top Hanako-Nom/Acc beautiful thought
       'Taroo thought Hanako beautiful.'

The finite form of the adjective in (18a) can take either *ga* or *o*, whereas the non-finite form of the adjective in (18b) fails to co-occur with the subject marked by *ga*. Examples like (18b) are viewed as adjectival small clauses, the subject of which is exceptionally case marked by a matrix predicate. According to Takezawa, a relationship between *ga* and finiteness suggests that the subject in modern Japanese moves to Spec(IP).

In OJ, the predicates *fori* 'want' and *fosi* (the adjectival counterpart of *fori*) take a non-finite adjectival small clause as their complement, in a similar way to (18b).[5] This is illustrated in (19a, b).

(19) a. [s [aka-kinuno fitura-no koromo] nagaku] fori (M. 2972)
        scarlet   lining-Gen dress   long want
        '(I) want a dress of scarlet lining to be long.'
   b. [s [wa-ga inoti-**no** (之)] nagaku] fosi (M. 2943)
        I-Gen life-Subj   long   want
        'I want my life to be long.'

The subject of the adjectival predicate *nagaku* 'long' can be either unmarked as in (19a) or marked by *no* as in (19b). This supports the view that the subject in OJ is licensed independently of Tense. Furthermore, the verbs *omofi* 'think' and *wosi* 'regret' take a clause containing a predicate suffixed by *ku*, as illustrated in (20a-c). (It is widely known among traditional grammarians that the suffix *ku* serves to nominalize the predicate that it attaches to.)

(20) a. [s mutsubisi fimo-**no** (乃) tokura-ku] omofe-ba...(M. 4427)
        tie lace-Subj   loosen-Suf think-when
        'When I think my dress-laces that he tied get loose...'

---

[5] The OJ examples are taken from *Manyoshu*, an anthology of Japanese verse completed early in the ninth century. It was originally written with so-called *Manyogana*; or Chinese characters used to phonetically represent Japanese sounds. Later editions were transcribed with *Kanji* 'Chinese characters' and *Kana* 'Japanese phonetic characters'. To get data as precise as possible for case markings in *Manyoshu*, I referred to the original text called *Nishi Honganji Bon*. The *Kanji* used for particles are taken from the original text and written in parenthesis in each example. Polyphonic differences in OJ are irrelevant in this study and hence completely ignored. The transliterations used in the examples are based on Nakanishi (1981).

b. [_S tsato-**no** (乃) kakura-ku] wosimo (M. 1205)
   home-Subj recede-Suf sad
   'I am sad that my home recedes from sight.'
c. [_S ume-no fana tirama-ku] wosimi (M. 824)
   plum-Gen blossom fall-Suf regret
   '(They) regret the plum-blossoms falling down.'

Given that a finite subordinate clause requires a subordinate marker such as *to* 'that', as in (18a), I assume that the subject and the predicate with *ku* in (20a-c) form a nominal small clause. The view that a *no*-marked NP and a predicate with *ku* form a subject-predicate relation rather than the genitive *no* modifying the following nominal predicate is supported by the fact that a predicate with *ku* can freely take an unmarked subject, as evidenced by (20c). Examples (19) and (20) indicate that the subject in OJ is licensed inside a small clause without being case-marked by the matrix predicate. It must be noted, however, that the subject of a small clause is generally marked by *no*, and that a *ga*-marked subject is rarely found in a small clause (see Koji 1988).[6] This may suggest that *ga* in OJ is licensed by Tense in the same way as in MJ. A problem is that if *ga* is licensed by Tense in the same way as in MJ, it is not clear why *ga* in OJ behaves differently from *ga* in MJ. *Ga* in OJ differs from *ga* in MJ in that 1) it appears in embedded clauses, but not in matrix clauses with a predicate in the conclusive form (cf.Sasaki 1996), 2) *ga* is used as a genitive particle modifying

---

[6] There are, however, some instances in which the subject marker 之 is glossed as *ga* with the *ku*-predicate, as in (i).
  (i) [Kimi-ga (之) finikeni oyuraku] wosimo (3246)
      lord-Subj from day to day older regrettable
      'I regret the lord is getting older from day to day.'
Note, however, that the graph 之 is ambiguous in that it can also be read *no*. Traditional grammarians generally believe that the use of *ga* and *no* is determined by the semantic properties of the subject NP; that is, *ga* tends to be used for the NP that denotes a person and expresses 'closeness', 'intimacy', etc. in a given discourse context and *no* is used otherwise (see, for example, Ohno 1977). In my view, these particles differ in structural position and discourse-related semantic meanings are assigned to the resulting configuration. Thus, in examples like (i) 之 should be glossed as *no*, based on the fact that *ga* rarely appears in small clauses.

the following noun phrase, and 3) the canonical *ga-o* transitive pattern in MJ is not found in OJ. (A more detailed empirically informed discussion will be given in section 4.4.)

Finally, the lack of TP in OJ may be supported by the fact that OJ has no derived subject marked by *ga* or *no*. Consider the passive construction in *Manyoshu* in which the passive morpheme *ru* or *yu* is attached to the verb.

(21) a. na-ga fafa-ni kora-re a-fa yuku (M. 3519)
 you-Gen mother-by scold-Pass I-Top go
 'Scolded by your mother, I go away.'
 b. wa-ga tuma-**fa**...yo-ni watsura-re-dzu (M. 4322)
 I-Gen wife-Top world-by forget-Pass-Neg
 'My wife...will not be forgotten by the world.'
 c. tewono tora-e-nu (M. 1403)
 axe take-Pass-Aux
 'My axe was taken away.'

Koji (1980) observes 49 examples of passives in *Manyoshu*. Most of them occur with the agentive phrase marked by *ni* as in (21a), but no subject marked by *ga* or *no* ever appears in a passive sentence. There are a few examples in which a subject is marked by the topic *wa* as in (21b) or in which a subject lacks a case marker as in (21c).[7] Assuming that the derived subject is licensed in TP, the absence of case-marked subjects in the passive construction favors the view that they fail to move to Spec(TP). From the OJ data discussed above, there is no positive evidence for the existence of Tense, which makes it plausible to assume that OJ lacks the category Tense, on a par with OE, as discussed in section 4.2.1.

In section 4.2.2, I showed that there is a close link between *ga* and clause structure change in Japanese, and hypothesized that *ga* is a clausal head taking a VP complement. Considering the facts concerning small clauses

---

[7] The fact that unmarked subjects may appear inside small clauses shows that they can occur *in-situ*. Unmarked subjects can also appear in the topic position in main clauses.

discussed above, I propose that the categorial status of *ga* in OJ is Agr. *No*-marked subjects, on the other hand, are base-generated inside lexical projections such as AP, NP, or VP. It follows that small clauses in OJ involve no functional categories. This is represented in (22a, b).

(22) a. [$_{\text{AgrP}}$ NP ga [$_{\text{VP}}$ ...V]]
     b. [$_{\text{XP}}$ NP-no X]

In (22a), *ga* is the head of AgrP that selects a VP complement, and the subject NP appears in Spec(AgrP).[8] (22b) is the structure of small clauses, in which the subject appears inside a lexical projection.[9] Further empirical arguments for the difference in categorial status between *ga* and *no* are given in the following sections.

The view that *ga* is the head of AgrP provides a straightforward explanation for the well-known fact that *ga* does not occur with the conclusive predicate in main clauses. Nomura (1993, 1996) observes that in OJ, case-marked subjects can appear in matrix clauses with a phrase marked by *ka*. Importantly, when they appear in the same clause, a phrase marked by *ka* must precede a case marked subject, as illustrated in (23).

(23) idukuni-**ka** (加) kimi-**ga** (之) fune fate kutsa mutsubi-kemu (M. 1169)
      which-Q   you-Subj   ship stop grass tie-Past
      'Which (port) did your ship cast anchor at?'

According to Nomura (1993, 1996), there are about 90 examples in *Manyoshu*

---
[8] Chomsky (1995) proposes to eliminate the category Agr on the assumption that Agr carries only uninterpretable features and that the presence of Agr cannot be justified as part of the clause structure. For present purposes, however, I propose that subjects with *ga* in OJ appear in Spec(AgrP) and do not move to Spec(TP).

[9] As opposed to full clauses, it was originally proposed that small clauses are maximal projections of their predicates and do not involve any functional projection (cf. Stowell 1983, Chomsky 1981). More recently, there have been various proposals for the categorial status of small clauses, many of which include the functional projection AgrP (cf. Chomsky 1989, Raposo and Uriagereka 1990 and others).

in which *ga/no*-marked subjects are preceded by *ka*-marked phrases, whereas there are only 5 examples in which subjects precede *ka*-marked phrases.[10] Watanabe (2002) takes this fact to argue that OJ possesses overt *wh*-movement. From the *Manyoshu* data examined in this study, it seems that the same ordering restriction holds for non-interrogative focus phrases with a *kakari*-particle. This is illustrated in (24a, b).

(24) a. nageki-**so** (曽) a-ga (我) suru (M. 3524)
　　　sigh-Foc　　　I-Subj　　do
　　　'I heave a heavy sigh.'
　　b. fanatatibana-wo (乎) tama-ni-**so** (曽) a-ga (我) nuku (M. 3998)
　　　mandarin-Obj　　　string-on-Foc　　I-Subj　　string
　　　'I will string on string the mandarin of my yard.'

I hypothesize that *kakari*-focus particles such as *so* and *ka* head CP. Examples (23) and (24) then have the structure given in (25).

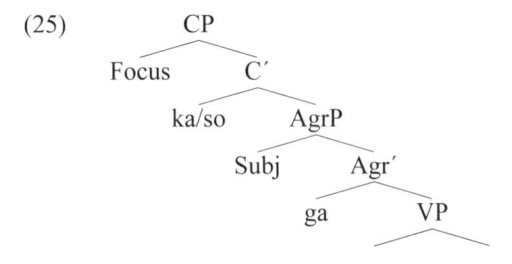

(25)　　　　　CP
　　　　　　／＼
　　　　Focus　　C′
　　　　　　　　／＼
　　　　　ka/so　　AgrP
　　　　　　　　　／＼
　　　　　　　Subj　　Agr′
　　　　　　　　　　／＼
　　　　　　　　ga　　VP

Given that the focus particle heads CP and *ga* heads AgrP, the word order restriction between these elements follows naturally. Importantly, these particles play a key role in clause structure change in Japanese, which is accounted for by the theoretical assumption that structural change of a clause

---

[10] In all five cases listed in Nomura (1993), subjects that precede *ka*-marked phrases are marked by *no*, which in turn indicates that *ga*-marked subjects necessarily follow *ka*-marked phrases. I will later argue that *no*-marked phrases that precede a *wh*-phrase involve topicalization rather than subjectivization.

starts out with a simple change in the abstract feature of its head. I have discussed morphosyntactic change of a clause headed by *ga* in section 4.2.2. I will argue in 4.7.1 that the clause initial *ka* in OJ and the clause final *ka* in Modern Japanese bear a structural relation in which the former c-commands the latter. Under the head initial hypothesis, it will be suggested that *ka*, as a clitic, is base-adjoined to the auxiliary verb (cf. Chapter 3), and has a strong [+Foc] feature in OJ. The [+Foc] feature triggers overt Q-movement in *wh*-interrogatives. The [+Foc] feature of *ka* was lost, and consequently, *ka* stays *in-situ* in Modern Japanese.

Note that OJ has two kinds of focus particles: *kakari*-focus particles, such as *so* and *ka* and adverbial focus particles, such as *sae* and *sika*. *Kakari*-particles differ crucially from adverbial focus particles in that they are sensitive to "clause-type," indicating questions, exclamatives, uncertainty, doubt, etc. Furthermore, while *kakari*-particles do not appear inside adjuncts and complex NPs (cf. Yamada 1938), adverbial focus particles can appear freely inside these island clauses, as illustrated in (26a-c).

(26) a. [NP yama-**safe** fikari saku fana]… (M. 477)
mountain-even shining bloom flower
'A blooming flower that shines bright even over the mountain'
b. [NP faru-fi-**sura** ta-ni tati tukaru kimi]-wa kanasi-mo (M. 1285)
spring-day-even field-in stand tired you-Top sad
'You, the lord who get fatigued standing in the field even on spring days look sad.'

The fact that the adverbial focus particles can occur inside the island clause shows that they appear in a position lower than *kakari*-focus particles.

Rizzi (1997) hypothesizes that a CP is split into several independently motivated subcategories, each of which heads its own projection. A sentential type operator resides in what he calls Force, which specifies 'clause-type' or mood. Force is an obligatory category in the highest layer within CP. Topic and Focus are optional categories and reside in the lower layers in the C-system.

From the observations concerning adverbial focus particles as in (26a, b), discussed extensively in Chapter 2, I assume that FocP appears in a position lower than a CP. I suggest that *kakari*-focus particles and adverbial focus particles belong to the category Focus, but that only the former move to the domain of CP in order to check the mood (or 'clause type') features. While *kakari*-dependency ('focus concord' constructions) is completely lost in Modern Japanese, many of the adverbial focus particles remain throughout the history without much change in their semantic contents. Since the category Focus is completely optional and does not select any category, adverbial focus particles never affect clause structure change. *Kakari*-focus particles, on the other hand, appear in Comp and select clausal complements; hence, they crucially affect clause structure change in the history of Japanese.

There is a large growing body of literature which argues for a strong correlation between the rise of nominative *ga* and the loss of *kakari*-focus particle *so* (cf. Yanagida 1985, Adachi 1992, Ohno 1977, 1993, Nomura 1996, Yamada 2001). Ohno (1993) examined the occurrence of *ga* and *so*, by comparing the Tale of *Heike* and the later text of *Heike*, known as *Amakusa Heike* (cf.4.2.2). He observes that the subject is frequently marked by the focus particle *so* in the Tale of *Heike*, but that there are many instances in which the focus particle *so* is replaced by *ga* in *Amakusa Heike* (see also Yamada 2001). Under my analysis, this is represented in (27)[11].

(27) [XP so [$_{AgrP}$ NP no/ga [$_{VP}$...]]] > [XP$_i$ ga [$_{AgrP}$ t$_i$ [$_{VP}$...]]]

Suppose that a *kakari*-focus particle selects AgrP. Then it is easily imaginable

---

[11] Nomura (1996) indicates that while focus phrases marked by the *kakari*-particle must precede case-marked subjects in the Nara period (710-784) this word order restriction had already broken down in the *Heian* Period (784-1186), and that *ga/no*-marked subjects had started to appear in a position preceding a *kakari*-marked focus phrase. Nomura, however, gives no example that has this word order configuration in the *Heian* period. Given that the matrix use of *ga* was restricted to intransitive verbs in *Amakusa Heike* (cf. Section 4.2.2), it is quite doubtful that movement of *ga* had already taken place in the *Heian* period.

4 Case/Focus Particles and Clause Structure Change 105

that the particle *ga* came to be in competition with the *kakari*-focus particle *so* at some point in history and *ga* replaced *so*. This can be viewed as loss of focus movement caused by a morphological change of these particles. I take this to mean that Japanese had undergone a diachronic shift from a "focus prominent" language to a "subject prominent" language. (See Lehmann (1976) for this typological shift.)[12]

Although study of the case particle *ga* in Old Japanese (OJ) has received a great deal of attention among traditional Japanese grammarians, no research has ever been conducted on the distribution of *ga* with respect to the position of objects in the same clause. This is because Japanese is a pro-drop language and many transitive clauses in OJ texts never contain overt arguments. In order to investigate the clause structure of OJ, I examined two representative texts written in the Nara period (710-784): *Manyoshu* (Collection of Myriad Leaves) and *Konkoumyou Saishou Oukyou* (The Sutra of Golden Light).[13] I extracted all instances of transitive clauses whose subjects and objects are overtly expressed, and in the following section, I show that transitive clause structure in OJ differs significantly from that in MJ.

---

[12] Lehmann (1976), following the typological studies advanced by Li and Thompson (1976), held that many Indo-European languages including English developed from topic-prominent into subject-prominent languages (see also Lehmann 1974, Hock 1986, 1992). Although Modern English possesses topicalization such as 'the man in a white shirt, I don't like', it does not belong to topic prominent nor focus prominent languages. Likewise, I do not take present-day Japanese as a focus prominent language even though morphologically marked focus phrases appear in FocP. I assume that focus prominent languages are those in which focus phrases move obligatorily in the overt syntax.

[13] *Konkoumyou Saishou Oukyou* (The Sutra of Golden Light) is the most popular Buddhist sutra in Japan. It was originally written in India and was translated into Chinese in 703. This Chinese text was read in Japanese through a system called *haku ten* 'white markings' on the original Chinese text.

4.4 Word Order in Early Old Japanese

4.4.1 The Basic Word Order Pattern

In OJ, arguments in the main declarative clause tend to appear without a case particle, while those in the embedded clause manifest overt case morphology. This is illustrated in (28a, b).

(28) a. Nanifa-no miya-ni wago ookimi kuni sirasu-rasi (M. 933)
   Naniwa-Gen court-Loc my emperor country govern-Aux
   'In the Naniwa Court, the emperor might govern the country.'
   b. [Umi-no soko oki kogu fune-**wo** (乎)] feni yose-mu
   sea-Gen bottom offing row ship-Obj neighborhood bring-Aux
   kaze-mo   fuka-nu-ka (M. 1223)
   wind-Foc blow-not-Q
   'Does wind not blow so as to invite the ship far from the offing out on the sea?'

In (28a) both the subject and object are left morphologically unmarked. In (28b) the object that appears in the embedded clause is marked by the particle *wo*. Miyagawa (1989) observes that while *wo*-marked objects in OJ need not appear adjacent to the verb, objects lacking a case particle must occur immediately adjacent to the verb.

In *Manyoshu*, I found 88 examples in which subjects are marked by the case particle *ga* or *no* and objects appear unmarked (cf. Yanagida 2003a, b). Three representative examples are given in (29a-c).[14]

(29) a. wa-ga hi-no miko-**no** (乃) uma namete (M. 239)
   I-Gen sun-Gen prince-Subj horse ranging
   'Our Prince of the Sun, ranging his horses...'

---
[14] For more examples, see *Manyoshu* (20, 167, 1249, 1919, 2531, 2639, 2694, 2742, 2746, 2813, 3272, 3791, 3847, and others).

b. Sayofime-no ko-**ga** (何) fire furisi yama-no na (M. 868)
   Sayo-Hime-Gen dear-Subj scarf waved hill-Gen name
   'the name of the hill where Sayo-Hime waved her scarf'

c. idukuni-ka kimi-**ga** (之) fune fate kutsa mutsubi-kemu (1169)
   where-Q   you-Subj   ship stop grass tie-Past
   'Which port in the world did your ship cast anchor at?'

Examples (29a-c) illustrate canonical transitive clauses in OJ, in which subjects are marked by *ga/no* and non-overtly marked objects appear adjacent to the verb. Importantly, however, the canonical [subject-ga object-o V] pattern in Modern Japanese is not found in OJ. I will propose the following generalization in early Old Japanese.

(30) Word Order in Early Old Japanese
  (i) Morphologically unrealized objects must stay *in-situ* (SOV).
  (ii) Objects marked by *wo* must move over a subject (OSV).

When subjects are case-marked, objects must appear morphologically unmarked, resulting in SOV order. When objects are marked by *wo*, they are raised over a subject, resulting in OSV order. This indicates that *wo* shows up obligatorily when objects are moved outside a VP.

There are, however, a few problematic cases that appear to be counterevidence to (30ii). Note first that examples that have the configuration [$_S$ NP$_i$-ga/no [$_S$ pro$_i$ NP-wo V] V] as in (31) do not count as a [subject-ga/no object-wo] pattern since in this configuration there are two arguments: the subject and the object, but they occur in different clauses; the subject in the main clause and the object in the subordinate clause.

(31) wagimoko-**ga** (之)[ware-**wo** (吾呼) okuru-to]...nakisi
   my-maid-Subj   I-Obj   see off that sob
   omofoyu (M. 2518)
   remember
   'I remember my pretty maid sobbing loud, when she was seeing me off.'

In (31), the subject of the embedded clause is a phonologically empty *pro* coindexed with the subject in the main clause. Now consider (32).

(32) tsoko-mo-ka fito-**no** (之) [wa-**wo** (乎) koto]
   that-Foc   people-Subj   I-Obj   say
   natsa-mu (M.512, 1329,1376)
   do-Aux
   'People say this and that of me.'

In (32) has a mono-clausal structure, it is clearly counterevidence to (30ii). Note, however, that in (32) the word *koto* 'talk' is a verbal noun and *natsu* is the light verb that corresponds to *suru* 'do'. The object NP is not selected by the verb *natsu*, but by the verbal noun *koto*. Given that (32) is an instance of the light verb construction, the sentence has the structure in which the object NP forms a constituent NP with the verbal noun that follows it. If this is the case, (32) has the same pattern as (29a-c).(For light verb constructions, see Grimshaw and Mester 1988, Miyagawa 1989 and many others.)
   Let us now consider (33).

(33) Sayofime-**ga** (何) kono yama-no ufe-ni fire-**wo** (遠) furi-kemu (M. 872)
   Sayohime-Subj   this hill-Gen up-Loc   scarf   wave-Aux
   'Sayohime waved her scarf upon this hill.'

(33) is a simple transitive clause with the case marked arguments. It is important to note that *Manyoshu* is written with a mixture of the Chinese characters used to phonetically represent Japanese sounds (i.e., *Manyogana*) and those that

represent words rather than sounds. The character 遠 conveys the meaning 'far away' when used as a word. This character can be used as *Manyogana* and it is phonetically read *wo*. This phonetic form is translated as the morphological case in (33). But note that the same phonetic form *wo* is often used for the word 緒, which means 'long cloth'. (33) can then be read in a way that *wo* together with *fire* 'scarf' is interpreted as 'long scarf' rather than the noun *fire* 'scarf' with the case particle *wo*. If this is the case, (33) has canonical SOV order with a morphologically unrealized object. Since *Manyoshu* is written with *Manyogana*, there arise potential ambiguities in the interpretation of the Chinese characters. Once we establish a highly restrictive and principled grammar of OJ, it is possible to give a different interpretation than the one assumed in the traditional literature. Let us now turn to (34).[15]

(34) [wagimoko-**ga** (之) ikanito-mo wa-wo (吾) omofa-ne-ba] fufumeru
my-maid-Subj   anything-Foc   me   think-Neg-because closed
fana-no fo-ni tsakinu-besi (M. 2783)
flower-Gen ear-Loc bloom-Aux
'Because my maid pays me no heed, I should be ready to bloom like flowers.'

It is important to note that the character 之 used for the subject *wagimoko* can be read in three different ways: the case markers *ga*, *no* or the adverbial focus particle *si*. It is read *ga* in the traditional literature, as in Nakanishi (1980). However, aside from the fact that [subject-ga/no object-wo V] patterns do not exist in OJ, there is reason to believe that 之 in (34) is read *si* rather than *ga*. As illustrated in (35a, b), when the focus particle *si* is used in the embedded clause, it is predominantly used inside *ba*-clauses (cf. Koji 1988:583).

---

[15] In example (34) the personal pronoun in the object position is not written with *Manyogana*, but with the character 吾 that represents the word 'I'. When this character is used, the case particle is often absent in the original text *Nishi Honganji Bon*, but added in the later editions transcribed with a mixture of *Kanji* 'Chinese character' and *Kana* 'Japanese native word'.

(35) a. [futari-**si** (之)wore-ba]....tuki-wa tera-dzu tomo yosi (M. 1039)
two people-Foc be-because moon-Top shine-not fine
'Because we two are together, it matters little if the moon shines.'
b. [tuki-**si** (之) are-ba] aku-ramu waki-mo sira-dzu-site (M. 2665)
moon-Foc be-because dawn-Aux difference-Foc know-not-do
'Because there was a bright moon, I could not discern it was break of day.'

According to Koji (1988), there are 194 examples of the particle *si* inside embedded clauses, most of which appear in *ba*-clauses. Furthermore, when the subject is marked by the focus particle *si*, it can be followed by the case-marked object and in the matrix clause, *si* takes the predicate in the conclusive form, as in (36a, b) (cf. Sasaki 1996).

(36) a. imo-**si** (志) a-**wo** (乎) mati kanete nageki-tsu rasi-mo (M. 3147)
maid-Foc   I-Obj   wait hard   grief-do may-Excl.
'Maybe my maid is having a hard time waiting for me, heaving a sigh of dole.'
b. wagimoko-**si** (之) a-**wo** (乎) omofu rasi (M. 3145)
my maiden-Foc   I-Obj   think may
'My maiden may be longing for me.'

(36a, b) are not treated as a canonical transitive sentence, but they have the structure in which the subject marked by the focus particle *si* moves overtly to the domain of a CP, where it is assigned focus interpretations. It is then natural to assume that 之 in (34) is read *si* rather than *ga*. The subject marked by *si* in (34) may appear inside the *ba*-clause, as is generally assumed. It can possibly appear in the matrix clause and is associated with the predicate *besi* in the conclusive form, in which case, (34) is translated as 'although my maid pays me no heed, he should be ready to bloom like flowers'. (Note that the concessive reading of *ba* with the predicate in the *Izenkei* 'perfect form' is possible in early OJ.)

4 Case/Focus Particles and Clause Structure Change 111

The following example is also problematic in that the subject is marked by *no* and the object by *wo*.[16]

(37) ifebito-**no** (之) idura-to ware-**wo** (乎) tofa-ba ikani ifa-mu (M. 3689)
      family-Subj   where-that I-Obj   ask-if how say-Aux
      'If his family asks me where you are, what shall I say to them

Before we get into the discussion of (37), let us first consider (38a, b).

(38) a. [kimi-ga tukahi-**no** (乃)] mire-do aka-zara-mu (M.499)
        you-Gen messenger-Obj see though tire-Neg-seem
        'How many times I see your messenger, I don't get fed up with him.'
     b. [waga fimo-no wo-**no** (乃)] yufu te tayusi-mo (M.3183)
        my lace-Gen cloth-Obj   tie hand weary Exl.
        'How weary I feel my hand tying the laces!'

Motohashi (1995) observes that in OJ there are some instances in which the object NP of transitive clauses is marked by the genitive *no*. In (38a), the *no*-marked phrase is interpreted as the object of both the matrix and the embedded clauses. I speculate that in (38a) the *no*-marked object is moved from inside the matrix VP and the embedded clause contains a null pronoun coindexed with the *no*-marked phrase. This is represented in (39).

(39) NP-no$_i$ [e$_i$....V] t$_i$ V

In this configuration, it is natural to assume that the particle *no* is interpreted as a topic. (For more detailed discussion of the topicalization of *no*-marked phrases, see 4.5.) Given that *no* can mark the object in OJ, example (37) has exactly the same derivation as the one given in (39). The *no*-marked NP is the object of the matrix verb *ifu* 'say', and moves to the sentence initial topic

---
[16] Example (37) is pointed out to me by S.-Y Kuroda.

position. (Note that the dative object of the verb *ifu* 'say' is marked by *wo* in
OJ.) Finally consider (40).

(40) [mitsago wiru tsu-ni wiru fune-**no** (之) yufusifo-**wo** (乎)
 osprey be seashore-Loc be ship-Subj evening-tide-Obj
 matu-ramu yori]-fa ware-koso matsare (M.2831)
 wait-Aux than-Top I-Foc wait more
 'I am waiting (for you to come) more than a ship waiting for evening
 tides, driven against the seashore where some ospreys are feeding.'

(40) is an instance of head internal relative clauses (HIRCs) in which the head
noun phrase occurs within the relative clause. As Kuroda (1992) pointes out,
HIRCs are possible only when they are pragmatically related to the matrix
clause. He proposes the following condition on HIRCs.

(41) The Relevancy Condition: For [an HIRC] to be acceptable, it is
 necessary that it be interpreted pragmatically in such a way as to be
 directly relevant to the pragmatic content of its matrix clause (Kuroda
 1992).

Given that the *no*-marked phrase of HIRCs is pragmatically related to the
matrix clause and the particle *no* is associated with the topic, it is possible that
the *no*-marked phrase in (40) is moved to Spec(CP) within the relative clause.

4.4.2 Obligatory Movement of *Wo*-Marked Objects

Although the [subject-ga/no object-wo V] pattern is not attested
in *Manyoshu*, except for a few problematic cases listed above, I found 54
examples in which objects marked by *wo* precede subjects which are either
marked or unmarked. This means that the object that appears with a case
particle is necessarily raised over a subject. Examples (42a-c) represent OSV

---
[17] For more examples, see *Manyoshu* (2467, 2617, 2737, 3151, 3304, 3329, 3459, 3467, 3482, and others).

order.[17]

(42) a. [yama-no fa-ni itsayofu tuki-**wo** (乎)] ituto-**kamo** (母) wa-ga (吾)
      moutain-Gen edge-Loc linger moon-Obj when-Foc   I-Subj
      matiwo-ramu (M.1084)
      wait-Aux
      'I am waiting for the moon that lingers behind the mountain, wondering when it will appear.'
   b. ware-**wo** (乎) yami-ni-**ya** imo-ga (我) kofitutu   aru-ramu (M. 3669)
      I-Obj   dark-Loc-Foc maid-Subj long for   be-Aux
      'My maid may be long for me in the darkness.'
   c. a-ga te-**wo** (乎) koyofi-mo-**ka** tono-no wakugo-ga (我) torite
      I-Gen hand-Obj tonight-Foc master-Gen young-son-Subj hold
      nageka-mu (M. 3459)
      grieve-Aux
      'My master's son may hold my hand this evening and heave a sigh of sorrow.'

As in (42a-c), the *wo*-marked objects appear most frequently in the *Kakari-musubi* 'focus concord' construction. Given that objects immediately adjacent to the verb are licensed inside a VP, I assume that *wo* is not a case maker in OJ (e.g. Hashimoto 1969), but it has only the semantic/pragmatic function (i.e., topic, focus, definiteness, etc.). Thus *wo* can appear not only with an object, but also with a locative PP, as in (43).

(43)   yoru-no ime-ni-**wo** (越) tugite mie koso (M. 807, 3108)
       night-Gen dream-Loc-Foc always see-Excl
       'In my dream at night, I wish I could always see that.'

I propose that *wo*-marked objects in (42a-c) are obligatorily moved from inside a VP to the domain of CP. A question that needs to be addressed is what kind of semantic interpretation is assigned to the *wo*-marked phrases in (42a-c). Note that focus phrases marked by a *kakari*-particle are not iterative and there is only one *kakari* focus phrase per clause. The fact that a clause contains no more than one structurally represented focus is widely observed in other languages as well (cf. Kiss 1995). Given that *wo*-marked phrases precede *kakari*-focus phrases, I speculate that movement into the left peripheral position is an instance of topicalization. The OSV order as in (42) has the structure illustrated in (44).

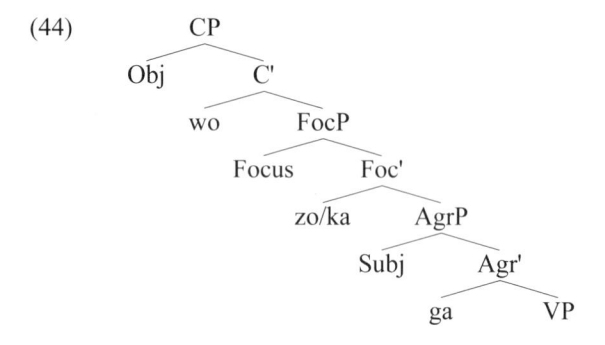

(44)
```
            CP
           /  \
         Obj   C'
              /  \
             wo   FocP
                 /    \
              Focus   Foc'
                     /    \
                   zo/ka   AgrP
                          /    \
                        Subj   Agr'
                              /   \
                             ga    VP
```

The particle *wo* may be part of the object NP, as is the case of *no*-marked subjects, but there is one piece of evidence that it may head a CP (see section 4.6.1). Recall that under my account, *kakari*-focus particles are elements of Foc and move to Comp to check its 'clause-type' feature. When the object is moved to CP, as in (44), the *kakari*-focus particle stays in Foc.

Objects with *wo* can also appear inside adjunct clauses or complex NPs, as in (45a, b) or in a position lower than *kakari*-focus particles as in (45c) (cf. Yanagida 2003a, b).

(45) a. Yamasiro-di-**wo** (乎) fito tuma-**no** (乃) uma-yori iku-ni... (M. 3314)
    Yamashiro-road-Obj other woman-Subj horse-by go-Conj
    'When other women's men go traveling on horseback to Yamashiro…'

  b. Akidu no-**wo** (叫) fito-**no** (之) kakure-ba... (M. 1405)
    Akizu field-Obj   man-Subj speak of-when
    'When a man speaks of the moorland of Akizu…'

c. nanisi-**kamo** kimi-ga tadaka-**wo** (乎) fito-**no** (之) tuge-turu (3304)
   why-Q   you-Gen appearance-Obj people-Subj tell-Aux
   'Why did people tell me how you saw?'

Unlike matrix clauses, the OSV order in adjunct clauses cannot be derived by raising the object to the domain of CP, because topicalization, in general, is not allowed inside adjunct clauses. I suggest that the objects in (45a-c) involve Object Shift and move to Spec(AgrP).

It is important to note that movement of objects in OJ differs from scrambling in that it is obligatory and has semantic consequences. Motohashi (1989) observes that *wo* in OJ tends to appear with definite/referential nouns, while non-referential indefinite nouns are generally unmarked. According to Motohashi, examples (46) and (47) show this contrast.

Definite vs. Indefinite
(46) a. sigeyama-no tanibe-ni ofuru yamabuki-**wo** (乎)...
       wooden mountain-Gen valley-Loc grow yellow-rose-Obj
       fikiuwete (M. 4185)
       transplant
       'transplant the yellow-roses that grow in the valley of the wooden mountain'
   b. fitomoto-no nadesiko uwesi tsono kokoro (M. 4070)
       one-Gen fringed pink plant this heart
       'the heart that planted a flowering pink'

Referential vs. Nonreferential
(47) a. komatu-ga sita-no kutsa-**wo** (乎) kara-tsane (M. 11)
       small pine-Gen under-Gen grass-Obj cut-Mood
       'Please cut the grass under the small pine.'
   b. Akami Yama kutsane kari tsoke... (M. 3479)
       Akami Mt.   grass   cut remove
       'Mt. Akami I mowed and cut all the grasses...'

The correlation between Object Shift and definiteness /referentiality is well known across languages. Laka (1993) observes that in Basque, VP external objects are DPs headed by the determiner *a*, while VP internal objects are simply NPs in that they do not appear with the determiner *a*. A correlation between definiteness and overt accusative case is also attested in Turkish (cf. Mahajan 1990, Enç 1991). Although Japanese is known to be a language lacking morphological means to express definiteness and referentiality, pronouns in OJ are necessarily definite and referential. Thus, if Motohashi's observation is correct, we expect that object pronouns obligatorily take the particle *wo*. I investigated all occurrences of pronouns in both subject and object positions, and the result was straightforward. (For a detailed discussion on pronominal forms in OJ, see section 4.6.1.) While subject pronouns are either marked or unmarked, object pronouns must be marked by *wo*.

The fact that objects with *wo* necessarily appear outside a VP is independently supported by Kato's (2002) observations concerning negations in OJ. According to Kato (2002), when negations are expressed by a discontinuous negative complex *e-V-zu*, objects can occur either inside or outside the negative complex, as in [(NP) e (NP) V-zu]. But when they take the particle *wo*, they must appear outside the negative complex. This is illustrated in example (48).

(48) Kaguyafime-**wo** e-tatakafi tome-**dzu** nari-nu   (Taketori)
      Kaguyahime-Obj Neg-fight keep-back-Neg do-Aux
      '(We) did not fight and keep back Kaguyahime.'

The observation that case-marked arguments never appear inside a negative complex in OJ supports my view that *wo* necessarily appears outside a VP.

4.5 Topicalization of *No*-Marked Phrases

In this section, I investigate the transitive clause in *Konkoumyou Saishou Oukyou* (The Sutra of Golden Light), the most popular Buddhist sutra in Japan, which appeared in the late eighth century. *Konkoumyou Saishou Oukyou* was originally written in India and was translated into Chinese in 703. This Chinese text was read in Japanese through a system called *haku-ten* 'white markings' which appeared on the original Chinese text, and were used as a way of translating Chinese into Japanese. What is crucial is that since these markings were added to the original text by Buddhists in the *Nara* Period (710-794), we are able to reconstruct the language of that period.

I have examined all instances of transitive clauses in *Konkoumyou Saishou Oukyou*. In this text, I found 39 examples of the configuration [$_S$ NP-no NP-wo V]. (The text used in this study is given in Kasuga 1943, reprinted in 1969.) (49a, b) illustrate the original Chinese text followed by the Japanese translation.[18]

(49) a. 善男子善女人 [… 入真理] 生信敬心 (Ch3-5:46)
yoki wotoko yoki womina-**no** [$_S$…sinri-ni ira-mu to] sin-no uyamafu
fine man good woman-Subj truth-into enter-Aux when faith respect
kokoro-**wo** umi…
mind-Obj bear
'Fine men and women attain the mind that respects faith when they enter into the truth.'

b. 善男子善女人 [為 [求 … 菩提] 故] 修三乗道 (Ch3-5:50)
yoki wotoko yoki womina-**no** [[$_S$ bodai-wo motomuru]-ga tame-no
Fine men fine women-Subj Bodhisattva-Obj search for-Gen for-Gen
yuwe-ni] Sanjyou-no miti-**wo** wosame-simu…
reason-for Sanjyou-Gen doctrine-Obj master-Aux
'Fine men and women master the doctrine of Sanzyo because they search for a Bodhisattva.'

Moreover, there are 11 examples in which *ga*-marked subjects precede *wo*-marked objects, 10 of which are such that *ga*-marked subjects are the first

---
[18] Since my purpose is to examine the clause structure of OJ, the precise reconstruction of the phonetic translation of Chinese words is not an issue.

and second personal pronoun, as illustrated in (50a, b).[19]

(50) a. 我所出語時 (Ch. 8:144)
wa-**ga** katari-**wo** idatsa-simu toki...
I-Subj talk-Obj make-Aux-when
'the time when I was made to speak a word.'
b. 汝能流布是妙経王 (Ch8:146)
na-**ga** yoku kono Myaugyau-wau-**wo** rufu-si...
you-Subj successfully this Myaugyau-wau-Obj propagate
'You propagated this Myoukyouou successfully.'

Recall that neither the *no-wo* pattern nor the *ga-wo* pattern is found in *Manyoshu*. Hence, an interesting question arises as to why these patterns are found in *Konkoumyou Saishou Okyou*. Note that the first and second personal pronouns in *Manyoshu* were written either in *Manyogana*, such as 安我 'I' and 奈我 'you', or in the Chinese characters that represent words, such as 吾 and 汝 respectively. A complication that arises as to these personal pronouns is that the words 吾 and 汝 are read either with a case particle, as in *a-ga* and *na-ga* or without a case particle, as in *are* and *nare*. The case particles may be absent in the original text, but were added in later editions of *Manyoshu*, transcribed with a mixture of *Kanji* 'Chinese characters' and *Kana* 'Japanese phonetic characters'. Given that 吾 and 汝 have two different forms in *Manyoshu*, I would like to suggest that *ga* used with the first or second personal pronoun in (50a, b) is neither a functional head nor a postposition, but that it is an inflected form of the pronoun already listed in the lexicon. Given that the *ga-wo* pattern is restricted to first and second personal pronouns in *Konkoumyou Saishou Okyou*, (50a, b) are not taken as counterevidence to the word order pattern in OJ. They

---

[19] There is one counter-example in which the subject NP takes *ga* and the object NP takes *wo*, given in (i).
(i) 我弟捨身 (Ch.10:192)
wa-ga wotofito-**ga** mi-**wo** tsutete...
my-Gen brother-Subj oneself-Obj sacrifice
'My brother sacrificed himself.'

are treated in the same way as the *no-wo* pattern as given in (49a, b), which is used not only with pronouns, but also with noun phrases in general. I suggest that the *no*-marked subjects in (49a, b) involve topicalization from inside the VP, as represented in (51). (Recall that *no* and a subject NP form a constituent PP, which is base-generated inside a VP. cf. (22)).

(51)　[$_{CP}$ NP-no$_i$ [$_{AgrP}$ NP-o [$_{VP}$ t$_i$ V]]]

Topicalization of *no*-marked subjects in this configuration is frequently found in *Konkoumyou Saishou Okyou*. This may be attributable to the fact that the language used in this text is a direct translation of Chinese, which is a typical "topic-prominent" language in that topicalized phrases always appear in sentence initial position (see also Li and Thompson 1976). The left peripheral *no*-marked subject in (51) reflects the word order in Chinese.

In *Manyoshu*, there are some cases in which *no*-marked phrases appear to involve topicalization (see examples (37-40)). Nomura (1993, 1996) observes that while *ka*-marked phrases predominantly precede case-marked subjects, there are some examples in which case-marked subjects precede *ka*-marked phrases. All five examples listed by Nomura (1993) are given below.[20]

(52) a.　nagaruru mizu-no (母)　okite-ni-ka (賀)　ara-masi (M. 197)
　　　 flow water-Subj　　　　deep-in-Q　　　　be-Aux
　　　 'The water would be flowing in a deepest stream.'
　　b.　wa-ga yado no　fanatatibana-no (乃)　itusi-kamo (毛)...
　　　 my garden-Gen mandarin-Subj　　　　　when-Q
　　　 tsono mi nari-namu (M. 1478)
　　　 that fruit bear-Aux

---

[20] Nomura included (52a), in which the particle that follows the subject is read *no* following *Nihon Koten Bungaku Taikei* (Complete Anthology of Japanese Classical Literature). But note that the character 母 in the original text is generally read *mo*, but not *no* (cf. Koji 1988), and, in fact, read *mo* in Nakanishi's (1981) transliteration of *Manyoshu*.

'When will the flowers of the mandarin-orange in our front garden bear fruit?'

c. Tukusi-fe-ni   fe mukaru   fune-no (乃) itusi-kamo (加毛)…
Tsukushi-Loc head-toward ship-Subj   when-Q
kuni-ni fe muka-mo
home-Loc bow turn-Aux (M. 4359)
'When will this ship that is heading toward Tsukushi turn her bow toward my home?'

d. firu toke-ba toke-nafe fimo-no (乃) wa-ga sena-ni afiyoru to kamo (可毛)
day untie-if untie-not lace-Subj   my man-Dat lie that Q
yoru toke yasuke (M. 3483)
night untie easy
'Though the lace of my dress is hard to untie by day, is it easy to untie at night, since my man comes to me and lies with me?'

e. imo-no mikoto-no (能) ware-wo-ba-mo ikani seyo-to-ka (可)…
my dear-Subj   I-Obj-Top   how make-that-Q
futari narabi wi katarafisi…(M. 794)
two side by side sit talk
'My dear, I wonder what she wanted, sit side by side with me and talk…'

Note that in all cases listed by Nomura, the preposed subjects are marked by *no*, which, in turn, means that *ga*-marked subjects cannot be preposed over *ka*-marked phrases. I take these examples to involve topicalization of *no*-marked subjects over *ka*-marked phrases.

    Based on a thorough survey of the two representative OJ texts, the particle *ga* differs significantly from *no* in that (1) while subjects with *ga* appear in the functional projection immediately above a VP, subjects with *no* originate inside a VP (cf. (22)), (2) while subjects with *ga* must stay *in-situ*, *no*-marked subjects can move to the sentence initial topic position, and finally (3) *no* used most widely for subjects is replaced by *ga* in MJ. All these facts suggest that the particles *no* and *ga* have different syntactic status, namely, *no* is simply a postposition, but *ga* is a clausal head that takes a VP as its complement. In the following section, I will provide further evidence for the existence of two kinds of particles in Japanese.

4.6 Head Initial Hypothesis for Functional Categories

4.6.1 Clitic Pronouns in Old Japanese

Another phenomenon which supports the view that some particles are clausal heads rather than postpositions comes from the fact that OJ has a morphologically distinct series of pronouns, which are reminiscent of those in Romance languages (cf. Kayne 1991). These are morphologically reduced forms known as clitics and full pronominal forms called "strong pronoun," as shown below:

(53)

	Strong pronouns	Clitics
1st	are	a
2nd	nare	na
3rd	—	si
It/that	sore	so

Strong pronouns behave like a noun phrase with respect to the case pattern in that they can appear unmarked, as in (54), or marked by a particle, as in (55). Clitic pronouns, on the other hand, must be necessarily marked, as in (56).

Strong Pronouns
(54) a. are (安礼) fimo toku (M. 3361)
         we/I   lace untie
         'We untie our laces.'
     b. nare (奈礼) wa-ga te furenana…oti-kamo (M. 4418)
         you   my hand touch-not   fall-Q
         'Will you fall… though my hand never touches you?'

(55) a. are-**wa** (安礼波) ita-ramu (M. 3428)
we/I-Top   come-will
'we will come (to you).'
b. nare-**mo** (奈礼毛) are-**mo** (安礼毛) yotiwo-so moteru (M. 3440)
you-also   I-also   children-Foc have
'Both you and I have children.'
c. are-**wo** (安礼乎) tanomete asamasi mono-wo (M. 3429)
I-Obj   dependent offensive thing-Excl.
'Although he made me dependent on him, he found me offensive.'
d. satofito-no are-**ni** (安礼迩) tuguraku (M. 3973)
villager-Subj I-to   tell
'Villagers tell me'
e. ware-**yori**-mo (和礼欲利母) madusiki fito (M. 892)
I-than-even   poorer person
'a person poorer than myself'

Clitic Pronouns

(56) a. kimi-mo wa-**mo** (余毛) afu to-wa nasi-ni (M. 2557)
you-also I-also   meet-that-Top without
'Both you and I, without meeting each other…'
b. na-ga fafa-ni kora-re a-**fa** (安波) yuku（M. 3519）
you-Gen mother-by scold-Pass I-Top go
'Scolded by your mother, I now go away.'
c. nageki-so a-**ga** (安我) tsuru（M. 3524）
sigh-Foc I-Subj   do
'I heave a heavy sigh.'
d. a-**wo** (安乎) watsuratsu-na (M. 3457)
I-Obj   forget-Neg
'I wish he wouldn't forget me.'

The co-occurrence restrictions between particles and clitics are indicated below.

(57) Co-occurrences between Particles and Type of Pronouns

	Strong Pronouns	Clitics
fa	+	+
mo	+	+
ga	-	+
wo	+	+
ni	+	-/+
no	-	-
yori	+	-

The clitics can occur with all types of *kakari*-particles and with the case particles *ga* and *wo*, but they fail to occur with the case particles *no* and *yori*.[21]

In order to account for the difference between strong and clitic pronouns, it is important to relate to one of the major contributions to the analysis of clitics, as found in Kayne (1991). Kayne has extensively studied clitic pronouns in Romance languages, suggesting that clitic pronouns are left-adjoined to the functional head Infl (or Agr):

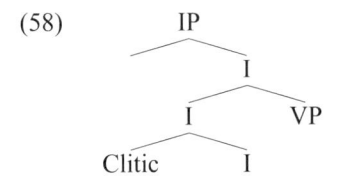

(58)
```
        IP
       /  \
          I
         / \
        I   VP
       / \
   Clitic  I
```

---

[21] I found 3 examples (3167, 3468, 3478) in which *ni* appears with clitics, but in all cases, it is used with the verb *yosu* selecting a *ni*-phrase, as in (i). Other verbs that take a *ni*-phrase occur with strong pronouns, as in (55d).
  (i) na-ni (奈尒) yotsori-keme (M. 3468)
      you-to   attract-Aux
      'I attracted to you.
Recall further that the subject pronoun must be in the form of a clitic with *ga*, suggesting that the clitic with *ga* is an inflected form of the pronoun already listed in the lexicon.

Following Kayne's (1991) analysis of clitics, Zwart (1991) indicates that clitic pronouns in Dutch move leftward, and argues that Infl precedes a VP in Dutch, contrary to the view that Dutch is a head final language (e.g. Koster 1975). An immediate inspiration for the view that clitics are left adjoined to some functional head is that we can now provide a principled account for clitic pronouns in OJ; namely *kakari*-particles and the case particles *ga* and *wo* head their own functional projections, and clitics are left-adjoined to these particles.[22] Consequently, the clause structure of OJ looks exactly like (58), as proposed in Kayne (1991). Table (57), however, indicates that the particles *no, yori, ni* do not occur with clitic pronouns. I take this fact to show that these particles are simply postpositions that form a constituent PP with the preceding NP.

4.6.2 Functional vs. Lexical Categories

Lightfoot (1991) demonstrates that reanalysis plays an important role in setting parameters, which may trigger large-scale syntactic changes. So, for example, Old English, like other Germanic languages, had underlying OV order and a verb moves to the "second" position in the main clause, known as the V2 effect. OV order, however, was reanalyzed as underlying VO at some point in the Middle English (ME) period. Old English differs from Dutch and German in that it had no obvious indicators for underlying verb position in main clauses. This resulted in decreasing the matrix instances of object-verb order and eventually resetting the parameter values. In other words, there was a change in the value of the directionality parameter. Within the antisymmetry framework of Kayne (1994), Roberts (1997) presents an alternative proposal for word order change in English. He argues that OV order in OE was derived from the VO base in conformity with Kayne's (1994) Linear Correspondence Axiom (LCA). What follows from the LCA is that VO order reflects the universal order while

---

[22] Since the case particle *wo* occurs with clitic pronouns, it may serve as a clausal head. But movement facts may show that the particle *wo* is part of the preceding NP. Note that objects with the particle *wo* appear in a particular structural position; namely AgrP or CP. Given that *wo* has [+Definite] features, and no case assigning properties, it can be the head of either Agr or Comp.

OV order is derived by leftward movement of the object over the verb. Loss of OV order is then comparable with loss of V-to-I movement in early Modern English. According to Roberts and Roussou (2003), this is caused by a change in the abstract feature of a functional head.

As it stands, the LCA makes it essential that OV languages like Japanese have functional categories that force overt movement of various categories. The elimination of the head parameter advanced by Kayne (1994), however, brings us a serious empirical problem as to how to characterize head final order in Japanese. The OJ texts examined above clearly show that unmarked objects immediately precede verbs. There is no evidence of underling verb-object order inside a VP. Likewise, particles strictly follow noun phrases. Note importantly that the case particles *yori* and *no* differ from *ga* and *wo* in that they fail to cooccur with clitics. The difference is also attested in the following examples in Modern Japanese.

(59) a. sono gakusei-**dake**-ni/kara
       that student only-to/from
    b. sono gakusei-ni/kara-**dake**
       that student-to/from -only
       'to/from only that student'

(60) a. sono gakusei-**dake**-wa/ga/o
       that student-only-Top/Nom/Acc
    b. *sono gakusei-wa/ga/o-**dake**
       that student-Top/Nom/Acc-only
       'Only that student'

The adverbial focus particle *dake* 'only' can appear either before or after the particles *ni* 'to' and *kara* 'from' as in (59a, b), but it fails to appear after *wa*, *ga* and *o*, as shown in (60b). I suggest that the particles *dake*, *ni* and *kara* differ from *ga* and *o* in that they are simply postpositions. Suppose that the particle *dake* is attached to the NP and the PP respectively in (59a, b). Then, the unacceptability of (60b) shows that the particles *wa*, *ga* and *o* do not form a constituent with the preceding NP.

From these empirical considerations, I maintain that the head parameter plays a major role in language variations, contrary to Kayne (1994). Since movement of the complement within lexical projections is not empirically attested, I propose that lexical projections have the head-final structure in Japanese, as shown in (61a, b).

(61) a. VP   b. PP
        / \   / \
       NP V   NP P

I make the following proposals concerning differences between functional and lexical categories.

(i) While the head parameter responsible for ordering variations is operative in lexical categories, functional categories are uniform with respect to the relative ordering between a head and a complement.
(ii) A functional category contains a specifier, but a lexical category does not (cf. Fukui 1986).
(iii) A specifier of functional categories is moved from within their complements.

Although this model is far less restrictive than Kayne's (1994) word order theory, it would vastly reduce the complexity of the derivation that head final languages like Japanese would face. The difference between lexical and functional categories with respect to their constituent order also has important implications for the nature of the language acquisition processes. From a learnability perspective, the ordering parameter reduces to the properties of lexical heads, i.e., operative only at the point of First Merge, combining a lexical head with its complement. This may be consistent with the view that parameterization is restricted to the lexicon (cf. Chomsky 1995, 2000). In other words, a parameter setting reduces to a facet of lexical learning, i.e., children set the value of the head parameter in a way that the verb is either followed or preceded by the object, which may come from the built-in Projection Principle and from the lexical entry for the verb.

Finally, since the proposed analysis eliminates the ordering parameter of functional categories, an optionality problem regarding scrambling, which has been much debated in recent years (cf. Fukui 1993, Miyagawa 1997, 2001), may not arise, and phrasal movement in Japanese is strictly stated in the light of the EPP-feature of functional heads, in accordance with the UG principles.[23]

4.7 Focus Projection and Clitic Q-Movement Revisited

In Chapter 2, I discussed the interaction between VP adverbs and focus elements, showing that FocP appears immediately above a VP. FocP also serves as an intervening category for *wh*-movement. This is illustrated in (62) and (63) respectively.

(62) a. John-wa Mary-sae/mo kibisiku sikatta.
     John-Top Mary-even/also severely scolded
     'John scolded even/also Mary severely.'
   b. ?*John-wa kibisiku Mary-sae/mo sikatta.
     John-Top severely Mary-even/also scolded

(63) a. ?*[$_{NP}$ dare-kara-no tegami]-sae/mo todoita-no?
     who-from-Gen letter even/also arrived-Q
     'Even/aslo a letter from whom has arrived?'

---

[23] Given that functional heads are invariably head initial, we may posit a covertly realized functional head F in the scrambling of PP as in (i).
  (i) [$_{PP}$ John-kara] F Mary-ga hon-o moratta.
       John-from   Mary-Nom book-Acc received
      'Mary got a book from John.'
Since this functional head has EPP-features, its specifier position must be filled by movement.

b. *Kimi-wa [$_{VP}$ nani-o kai]-sae/mo si-ta-no?
you-Top what-Acc buy-even/also do-past-Q
'What did you even/also buy?'

Examples (63a, b) show that the focus particles *sae* and *mo* are attached to the NP and the VP respectively, and that *wh*-elements are not allowed inside these constituents. I argued that (63a, b) have the structures given in (64a, b).

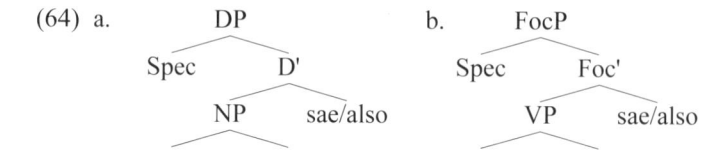

(64) a. DP   b. FocP
        / \   /   \
      Spec D'   Spec Foc'
           / \   /   \
          NP   sae/also   VP   sae/also

In the above head-final structures, the focus particles *sae* and *mo* are D and Foc respectively. Whatever other possibilities we might have for these particles, we run into a problem identifying their categorial status. Under the present hypothesis, the focus particles *sae* and *sika* are treated uniformly as Foc that takes a VP on their right, as represented in (65).

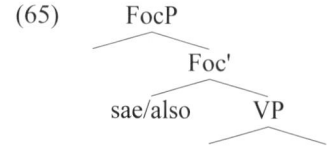

(65)   FocP
        / \
           Foc'
           / \
     sae/also VP

(62) and (63) are derived in such a way that the NP and the VP undergo 'generalized pied-piping' (Chomsky 1995:264) to the specifier position of *sae/mo*. The unacceptability of (63a, b) may indicate that the generalized pied-piping of the phrase containing a *wh*-word is not allowed because the heads *sae/mo* have [-Wh] features.

4.7.1 Clause Initial *Ka* vs. Clause Final *Ka*

In Chapter 3, I provided a number of empirical arguments for the view that *ka* is base-generated in Foc and that *wh*-questions in Japanese involve rightward Q-movement. Under the head initial hypothesis advanced in this chapter, it is predicted that there is no clause final complementizer in Japanese. This happens to be consistent with Fukui's (1986) claim that Japanese lacks overtly realized functional elements, in particular, D and C.[24] According to Fukui, the two elements *to* 'that' and the Q-particle *ka*, which are assumed to be complementizers, are in fact a postposition and a noun respectively. His arguments relate to facts concerning the distribution of various sequences of words. The view that *ka* is a noun is based on the distributional similarity between *ka* and *koto* 'fact', as illustrated in (66a, b).

(66) a. Bill-wa [NP [S John-ga sore-o katta] koto]-o sira-nai.
　　　 Bill-Top John-Nom it-Acc bought fact-Acc know-not
　　　 'Bill does not know (the fact) that John bought it.'
　　b. Bill-wa [NP [S John-ga nani-o katta] ka]-o sira-nai.
　　　 Bill-Top John-Nom what-Acc bought Q-Acc know-not
　　　 'Bill does not know what John bought.'

The verb *siru* 'know' selects a noun phrase as its complement in Japanese, and thus it is marked by the accusative particle *o*. The fact that a case particle is attached to *ka* constitutes evidence that *ka* is a noun. Furthermore, the topic particle *wa* takes a PP or an NP as its complement, as illustrated in (67a, b).

(67) a. [NP John]-wa Bill-o nagutta.
　　　 John-Top Bill-Acc hit
　　　 'John hit Bill.'

---

[24] Fukui (1986), however, takes the view that Japanese possesses defective Infl and that it is present only as a place holder for a tense morpheme such as *ta*. Chomsky (1995, 4.10), however, denies the presence of functional categories whose sole role is to create place holders. I assume that a verb is drawn from the lexicon fully inflected and that an inflected verb does not move to functional categories in Japanese.

b. [PP John-kara]-wa nagai aida tegami-ga ko-nai.
   John-from-Top long time   letter-Nom come-not
   'It is from John that letters have not come for a long time.'

The particle *wa*, but not *ga*, can occur with the clause selected by *to*, as illustrated in (68a, b).

(68) a. [[PP [S John-ga sono mondai-o toita] to] –wa] totemo omoenai
        John-Nom that problem-Acc solved that-Top inconceivable
        'It is inconceivable that John solved that problem.'
     b. *[[PP [S John-ga sono mondai-o toita] to] –ga] totemo omoenai
        John-Nom that book-Acc solved that-Nom inconceivable

The fact that the topic particle *wa* occurs only with a PP and an NP shows evidence that *to* is a postposition rather than a complementizer. Assuming with Fukui (1986) that *ka* is a noun, but not a complementizer, an important theoretical question arises as to how to account for the clause final *ka* in main clauses. In this connection, let us consider future tense auxiliaries in Croatian given by Wilder and Cavar (1994), as discussed in Chapter 3:

(69) a. *Citati-hocu knjigu.
        read will-1st book
     b. Citati-cu knjigu.
        read will-1sg book

(70) a. Ja hocu citati knjigu.
        I will-1sg read-Inf book
        'I shall read the book.'
     b. Ja cu citati knjigu.
        I will-1sg read-Inf book
        'I shall read the book.'

In the above examples, the future tense auxiliary *cu* is a clitic, a reduced form of its full counterpart, *hocu*. Wilder and Cavar (1994) argue that while the full auxiliary *hocu* may not be adjoined to the verb, the clitic *cu* is right-adjoined to the verb, as illustrated in (69a, b). It then follows that the order in (70b) shows that the clitic is excorporated from the verb, and possibly adjoined to a higher functional head. Assuming with Roberts (1991) that this kind of excorporation is possible in the case of head adjunction, let us now consider (71a-c).

(71) a. John-wa nani-o kai masita-ka?
    John-Top what-Acc buy-Aux-Q
 b. *John-wa nani-o katta-ka?
    John-Top what-Acc bought-Q
 c. John-wa nani-o katta-no?
    John-Top what-Acc bought-Q

In Chapter 3, I provided a number of arguments for the view that *ka* is a clitic. In (71a) *ka* is base-generated in Foc. The auxiliary verb moves from inside the VP and is left-adjoined to *ka*. The entire complex then moves to Comp. This rightward head movement, however, is in direct conflict with the assumption that functional categories are uniformly head-initial. One way to derive (71a) is to assume that the clitic *ka* is base-adjoined to the auxiliary verb *masu*, which is lexical, as illustrated in (72).

(72)   Aux⁰
           ╱   ╲
        Aux⁰   ka

The structure of (71a) is then represented in (73).[25]

---

[25] I assume that FocP is a functional category that appears above AuxP, and that it is instantiated whenever a clause contains an overt focus element.

(73)   CP
         ╱╲
        C   AuxP
            ╱╲
           VP   masu-ka

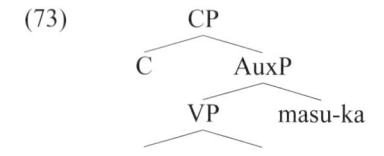

While *ka* in OJ heads CP and its EPP feature triggers overt movement of a (non)-interrogative focus phrase, *ka* in MJ is a pronominal clitic right-adjoined to the auxiliary verb and moves covertly to Comp. The ungrammaticality of (71b) shows that *ka* may not be adjoined to the empty Aux due to the condition in (74).

(74)   Stranded Affix Filter (Lasnik 1981)
       An affix must be a syntactic dependent of a morphologically realized category at surface structure.

Note that in OJ *ka* must appear adjacent to a *wh*-phrase, as shown in (75).[26]

(75)   idukuni-**ka** (加) kimi-ga (之) fune fate kutsa mutsubi-kemu (M. 1169)
       which-Q   you-Subj   ship stop grass tie-Past
       'Which (port) did your ship cast anchor at?'

Since the structure in (75) is lost in Modern Japanese, a question arises as to how to characterize change of *ka*-interrogatives. The structural difference between OJ and MJ can be accounted for in a principled way by the assumption that in (75) *ka* heads CP and clause final *ka* in MJ appears in Aux, which is lexical and c-commanded by Comp. I propose that the structural change of *ka*-

---

[26] I find no example in *Manyoshu* in which *wh*-questions in matrix clauses take clause final *ka*, but there are many instances in which clause final *ka* occurs in yes-no questions, as in (i)
   (i)   wa-ga furu tsode-wo imo mitu-ramu-ka (132)
         I-Subj wave sleeve-Obj dear see-Aux-Q
         'Would my dear have seen the sleeve I waved?'
I assume that in (i) *ka*, as a clitic, is base-adjoined to Aux and does not involve movement.

interrogatives is characterized as loss of focus movement reducible to change of abstract features associated with *ka*.

(76) The *Wh*-Parameter
    a. The structural change of *wh*-interrogative clauses is reducible to loss of the functional feature [+Foc] associated with *ka*.
    b. In OJ, *ka*-movement is obligatory in *wh*-questions, while in MJ it is prohibited.

I assume that covert *ka*-movement in MJ is driven not by focus features but by Q-features.

    Let us now turn to example (71c). The assumption that *no* is a complementizer base-generated in a Comp, as proposed in Chapter 3, does not hold under the head initial hypothesis. There is no right-headed Comp position. The distributional evidence suggests that *no* is a noun just like *koto* and *ka* in that it occurs with the verb *siru* and is marked by the accusative particle *o*, as in (76).

(77) Bill-wa [[s John-ga hon-o katta] no/koto/ka]-o sitteiru.
    Bill-Top John-Nom book-Acc bought that/Q-Acc know
    'Bill knows that John bought a book.'

If *no* is a noun just like *ka*, a question arises as to how to account for the contrast given in (71b, c), which will be discussed in the following section.

4.7.2 *No*-Interrogatives vs. *Ka*-Interrogatives

    Kuwabara (2001) suggests that *no*-interrogatives involve the phonetically unrealized sequence of the copula *desu* and the Q-particle *ka*, as shown in (78).

(78) John-ga nani-o katta no (desu ka)?
John-Nom what-Acc bought that be Q
'What is it that John bought?'

Putting aside Kuwabara's analysis of (78), I adopt his view that *no*-interrogatives contain a hidden sequence of *desu-ka*. Under my account, (78) has the complex structure represented in (79), in which the copula verb *desu* selects an NP headed by *no* and raises to Aux.

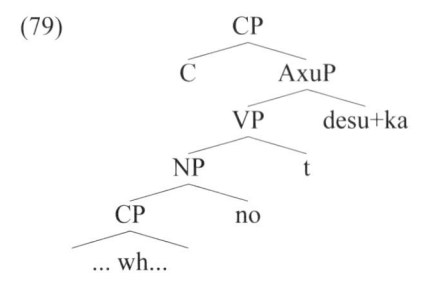

(79)
```
              CP
            /    \
           C     AxuP
               /     \
             VP     desu+ka
            /  \
          NP    t
         /  \
        CP   no
       /
    ... wh...
```

The clitic *ka* is base-adjoined to *desu*. As a clitic, *ka* is excoporated and moves covertly to the matrix Comp. Kuno's (1980) observations cited from Kuwabara (2001) may constitute evidence for my proposed analysis of *ka*-interrogatives and *no*-interrogatives.

(80) The focus domain of an interrogative complementizer is a constituent immediately preceding *ka*, unless it is contained in the nominalized clause of the *no-desu* construction.

Consider (81) and (82) cited from Kuwabara (2001) in relation to (80).

(81) a. Kono tokei-wa [**Pari-de** katta-no] desu-ka?
this watch-Top Paris-Loc bought-that be-Q
'Is it in Paris that you bought this watch?'

b. Kimi-wa [**syuusen-no toshi-ni** umareta-no] desu-ka?
   you-Top end-of war-Gen year-in born-that be-Q
   'Is it the year when the war ended that you were born?'

(82) a. ??Kono tokei-wa **Pari-de** kai-masita-ka?
   this watch-Top Paris-in buy-Past-Q
   'Is it in Paris that you bought this watch?'
   b. ??Kimi-wa **syuusen-no toshi-ni** umare-masita-ka?
   you-Top end-of-war-Gen year-in born-Past-Q
   'Is it the year when the war ended that you were born?'

In the above examples, the constituents in boldface are intended as the focus of the questions. (81a, b) can be interpreted in such a way that only the constituent in boldface is focused (i.e., narrow focus) and everything else is presupposed, while (82a, b) have only a wide focus interpretation in that the entire VP is focused. Thus, (83a) and (83b) can be the answers of (81a) and (81b) respectively, but not of (82a) and (82b).

(83) a. Hai, Pari desu.
   Yes, Paris be
   b. Hai, syuusen-no toshi desu.
   Yes, end-of-war-Gen year be

It is widely known that *ga* receives either an "exhaustive listing" or a "neutral description" reading. Diesing (1988) argues that the exhaustive listing *ga* corresponds to a narrow focus reading in that the constituent marked for focus may not project its focus; i.e., only that constituent itself receives a focus interpretation. A "neutral description" reading, on the other hand, gives a wide focus reading in which a constituent marked with focus may project its focus to the entire VP (cf. Chapter 2). Let us consider examples (84a, b), which are treated in the same way as (81) and (82).

(84) a. **John-ga** sono wain-o nonda-no?
John-Nom that wine-Acc drank-that
'Did JOHN drink that wine?'

b. ??**John-ga** sono wain-o nomi masita-ka?
John-Nom that wine-Acc drink-Past-Q
'Did JOHN drink that wine?'

While *ga* in (84a) is allowed to have an "exhaustive listing" reading, *ga* in (84b) is not. In other words, (84a) presupposes that someone drank wine and asks whether John is the one who drank wine. (84b), on the other hand, does not give rise to such presupposition. Diesing (1992) has proposed that elements with a narrow focus reading (i.e., constituent focus) involve movement either covertly or overtly, while those with a wide focus reading are interpreted *in-situ*. Suppose that a narrow focus reading is obtained by covert movement of a focus phrase. (For a more detailed account of semantic interpretations associated with focus movement, see Chapter 5.) We can provide a straightforward account for why the *ka*-interrogatives in (82a, b) and (84b) do not allow narrow focus interpretations.

In Chomsky (1995), the uninterpretable feature F of the target triggers a movement operation to eliminate it by checking. Suppose that the clause final *ka* moves covertly to check off the uninterpretable [+Q] feature in Comp. *Ka*-interrogatives do not allow covert focus movement, since the uninterpretable feature in Comp has already been checked and eliminated. As a result, in (82a, b) the focused phrase is interpreted *in-situ*, in the manner proposed in Diesing (1992). In contrast, given that *no*-interrogatives have the structure in (79), which contains a phonologically unrealized *desu-ka*, a higher Comp has the uninterpretable [+Q] feature, which triggers covert *ka*-movement, and the lower Comp has the uninterpretable [+Foc] feature, which triggers a covert movement of a focus phrase. The focus movement takes place within the c-command domain of the question operator and results in forming an independent operator-variable relation. The intended narrow focus interpretation is then acceptable in *no*-interrogatives.

Let us now turn to the particle *ka* in OJ. The particle *ka* in OJ appears in Comp in the overt syntax, and can host a non-interrogative focus phrase, as illustrated in (85).

(85) yama-wo asita-**ka** koe-i-namu (M. 3151)
 mountain-Obj tomorrow-Q cross-over-Aux
 'Is it tomorrow that (I) will cross over the mountain?'

In (85) the focused phrase moves overtly to the specifier position of *ka* and presumably has a narrow focus reading. This may raise a question of why covert focus movement is prohibited in *ka*-interrogatives in MJ. Note that the clause final *ka* is a noun (i.e., pronominal clitic) and as a noun it has an interpretable Q-feature. In contrast, *ka* in (85) is a functional head, which, by definition, carries an uninterpretable feature that must be eliminated by checking. I speculate that an interpretable Q-feature is intrinsic to *ka*, and that *ka* in OJ has an additional functional feature, namely, the uninterpretable focus feature that triggers focus movement. *Ka* in MJ, on the other hand, has no such feature. What this means is that the structural change of *ka*-interrogatives was caused by a change in the feature of *ka*, namely, loss of the uninterpretable functional feature [+Focus] associated with *ka*.

4.8 Summary

In this chapter, I have provided extensive discussion concerning clause structure change in the history of Japanese, highlighting, in particular, the syntactic properties of two kinds of particles. I have shown that the case particle *ga*, (possibly *wo*) and *kakari*-focus particles play a key role in change of clause structure in Japanese and suggested that these particles appear in the head of a clause that selects VP complements on their right. In this way, the structural change of a clause can be reduced to a simple change in the abstract feature of its head, following directly from the general principle of syntactic change recently proposed in the minimalist framework (cf. Whitman 2000, Roberts and Roussou 2003). From a number of empirical observations, however, other particles that do not contribute to clause structure change are likely to be postpositions and form a constituent PP with the preceding NP or S. Furthermore, I have shown that OJ possesses two types of objects. While objects *in-situ* are morphologically unrealized and immediately precede the verb, objects moved outside a VP necessarily appear with *wo*. Since constituent order inside a PP and a VP is strictly head-final and there is no evidence of underlying head-initial order, I take the view that while functional categories are invariably head-initial, the head parameter is operative in lexical categories. How the present line of the analysis is accommodated in the restrictive theory of phrase structure proposed in Kayne (1994) is left open to future research.

5

Focus Movement and Semantic Interpretation*

5.1 Introduction

Focus-background partition has been discussed under a number of different names (e.g. focus-presupposition, theme-rheme, topic-comment, old-new information, etc.) in a wide variety of works in the discourse/ pragmatic literature (cf. Givón (1979)). It has been widely acknowledged that focus-background is the informational structuring of sentences required by communicative purposes. The focus encodes what the sentence asserts and the background encodes what is already established in the given discourse context. While significant differences are found among different approaches, recent works in the area of formal semantics seem to share the view that the primary function of focus-background is not pragmatically motivated, but rather it is to provide a quantificational structure for focus sensitive operators.[1] The

---

* This chapter is a slightly revised version of my paper titled 'Focus Movement and the Quantificational Structure of Focus Sensitive Operators' which appeared in *English Linguistics* Vol. 20 (2003).

[1] Krifka (1988) proposes that focus-background provides a structured meaning equating to the <restrictor, nucleus> partition of quantification structures (see also Diesing 1992, Krifka 1995). Alternatively, Rooth (1985) proposes that a focused phrase provides a set of alternatives, which determines the domain of quantification for the operator that associates with a focused phrase.

communicative use of focus-background is understood as one of the properties of the resulting configuration.

The purpose of this chapter is two-fold. In the first half of this chapter, I will present an overview of the semantic theory of focus developed by Herburger (2000), who argues that focus restructures the quantificational structure of the event quantifier in that the non-focused material in its scope also contributes to its restriction. In the second half of this chapter, I will show that there are many cases in which the "Herburger-style" focus-affected reading never arises, and argue that the syntax plays a major role in the restructuring of the quantificational structure of focus sensitive operators. While Herburger proposes a mechanism in which focus is interpreted *in-situ*, I will provide an alternative movement account for the presence or absence of the focus-affected reading. My analysis is primarily based on Diesing's (1992) claim that semantic representations directly relate to syntactic representations. Diesing argues that there are two kinds of indefinites; non-quantificational indefinites are interpreted *in-situ*, whereas quantificational indefinites involve movement (see Chapter 2). Following Diesing's basic insight, I will present a number of empirical arguments supporting the view that "Herburger-style" focus affected interpretations arise only as a result of covert focus movement. I will argue that covert focus movement employs two structural positions: FocP and CP, on a par with *wh*-movement discussed in Chapter 2.[2]

5.2 Semantic Background

Within the framework of neo-Davidsonian semantics, it has been proposed in the literature that a sentence is understood as a description of events, and that all verbs are taken to denote one-place predicates taking an

---

[2] I assume that the structural realization of focus-background is subject to crosslinguistic variation. English resorts to covert focus movement, whereas languages like Hungarian resort to overt focus movement (cf.Kiss 1995). It is known that *wh*-movement shows the same variation.

event variable (e.g. Parsons 1990). Herburger assumes with Parsons (1990) that (1a) is translated as in (1b) rather than (1c).

(1) a. Brutus stabbed Caesar.
   b. ∃e (Stab(e) & Past (e) & Agent (e, brutus) & Theme (e, caesar))
   c. ∃e (Past (e) &Stab(brutus, caesar))

(1b) states that "there was a stabbing whose agent was Brutus and whose theme was Caesar." The arguments are treated in the same way as the adjuncts in that they are linked to the verb by conjunction. According to Parsons (1990), the view that both arguments and adjuncts form their own conjuncts accounts for the fact that arguments are not always obligatory elements of the verb. The theme of the verb *stab* in (1a) is purely optional, and there are many cases where two place predicates happen to take only one theta-marked argument and yet the sentences are completely acceptable:

(2) a. John ate fish.
   b. John ate.

(3) a. John studied math.
   b. John studied.

The separation of arguments into their own conjuncts is certainly desirable in representing the meanings of (2) and (3). Parsons (1990) further indicates that decomposition accounts for the logical entailment patterns illustrated in (4a-c).

(4) a. Brutus stabbed Caesar.
   b. Brutus stabbed Caesar in the back.
   c. Brutus stabbed Caesar in the back with a knife.

Note that both (4b) and (4c) entail (4a). If (4b) is true, then (4a) is also true. If (4c) is true, then both (4b) and (4a) are true. In other words, the longer sentences entail the shorter sentences. It is contradictory to assert the longer sentences and deny the shorter ones. This entailment pattern directly follows from the semantic representations of (4a-c), as given in (5a-c).

(5) a. ∃e (Stab(e) & Past (e) & Agent (e, brutus) & Theme (e, caesar))
   b. ∃e (Stab(e) & Past (e) & Agent (e, brutus) & Theme (e, caesar) & In-the-back(e))
   c. ∃e (Stab(e) & Past (e) & Agent (e, brutus) & Theme (e, caesar) & In-the-back(e) & With-a-knife (e))

Assuming that decomposition is radical enough to separate arguments into their own conjuncts, Herburger (2000) discusses how focus affects the quantificational structure of focus sensitive quantifiers.

One of the main aspects of Herburger's theory of focus is that focus is interpreted *in-situ* and the semantic effect of focus is obtained by the interpretive process called "focal mapping," as expressed in (6).

(6) Focal mapping
   The nonfocused material in the c-command domain of Q also provides an internal argument for Q.   (Herburger 2000:43)

Focal mapping is a process that takes LF representations as input, and makes the event quantifier Q binary in that it forms Q's internal argument translated as its restriction and Q's external argument as its scope.[3] For example, prior to focal mapping, the LF structure of (7) looks like (8a), where the event quantifier, represented as ~~sometime~~, is unary in that it has no internal argument, and becomes binary as in (8b) after focal mapping.

(7) PAUL ordered salmon.

---

[3] In Herburger's monograph, it is assumed that Q refers to quantifiers in general, which include both adverbial quantifiers such as *sometime, usually, always*, etc. and quantificational determiners such as *some, every, most*, etc.

(8) a. [~~sometime~~ [PAUL ordered salmon]]
 b. [[~~sometime~~ [ordered salmon]] [PAUL ordered salmon]]

The non-focused material inside the c-command domain of the event quantifier in (8a) ends up contributing to its restriction in (8b). (8b), then, is mapped into the "structured Davidsonian decomposition" in (9).

(9) [∃e: C(e) & Order(e) & Past(e) & Theme(e, salmon)] (Agent(e, paul) & Order(e) & Past(e) & Theme(e, salmon))

(9) contains the context predicate C that restricts events relevant to the context in which the sentence is used. Note that the restrictive clause in (9) only states that there exists some relevant past event of ordering salmon but not of someone's ordering salmon. Our understanding that there exists such a person who ordered salmon is not described as part of the semantics of the verb, but as part of our world knowledge; that is, events of ordering require an agent. Importantly, Herburger claims that the non-focused material in the restriction of Q is entailed by the sentence. In other words, (7) is about some past event of ordering salmon and entails that there was such an event in the past. She uses the term "backgrounded focal entailment" (Herburger 2000:20) to refer to entailments that appear in the restriction of Q.

5.3 Focal Presupposition to Entailment

Herburger presents a number of arguments against the view that (7) presupposes that someone ordered salmon. It is widely known that a presupposition is described as a proposition whose truth is taken for granted as part of the background of the conversation, and thus is a precondition for felicitous utterance of the sentence. Based on empirical considerations, however, presuppositions do fail. Under various nonstandard logics, in particular three-valued and supervaluational logics, the failure of presuppositions leads the sentence to have no semantic value. An important difference between the presuppositional analysis and Herburger's analysis is that her analysis retains a two valued semantics and that in case a "backgrounded focal entailment" fails, the sentence is not valueless, but is simply false. Let us now consider (10a, b).

(10) a. MANY OF HIS COLLEAGUES like Bill.
    b. NOBODY likes Bill.

Examples like (10a, b) are problematic under the presuppositional view that the non-focused part of a sentence expresses an existential presupposition. (10a), with the non-decreasing quantifier, presupposes that someone likes Bill, but (10b), with the decreasing quantifier, does not presuppose that someone likes Bill. By replacing presuppositions with entailments, Herburger provides a simple account for the difference between (10a) and (10b). Herburger claims that focal mapping applies after QR; that is, in (10a, b) the quantifiers undergo QR prior to focal mapping. The absence of the "backgrounded focal entailment" in (10b) is then accounted for by the view that the negative quantifier takes scope over the event operator. (10b) is translated in (11).

(11)   [nobody x] [∃e: C(e) & Like (e) & Theme (e, bill)] (Experiencer (e,x) & Like (e) & Theme (e, bill))
    'Nobody is such that some relevant event of liking Bill had him or her as its experiencer.'

(11) is now about whether Bill is liked. Since the negative quantifier takes scope over the existential event quantifier, (10b) does not entail that Bill is liked. The non-decreasing quantifier in (10a), on the other hand, does not cancel the existential import of the event quantifier. Let us turn to cases in which focus is embedded within an *if*-clause or a clause inside the verb *discover*:

(12) a. If HILLARY trusts Bill, all is well.
    b. Joan discovered that HILLARY trusts Bill.

In both (12a, b) even if the speaker does not believe that there exists someone who trusts Bill, the sentences do not become "valueless" (fail to be interpretable), but they are intuitively true. Under Herburger's analysis, the absence of the existential import is again accounted for by the scopal interaction between the existential event operator and higher illocutionary, attitudinal or epistemic predicates such as *if* and *discover*. In other words, "backgrounded focal entailments," which appear in the restriction of the event operator, can be suspended if a quantifier-like element appears in a position higher than the existential event operator.

5.4 Adverbs of Quantification

5.4.1 Association with Focus

I will now discuss how Herburger's theory of focus accounts for "adverbs of quantification" that have been extensively discussed in the literature since the term was first used by Lewis (1975). It is widely acknowledged that adverbs of quantification (henceforth Q-adverbs) associate with focus and that examples like (13a, b) have different truth conditions (cf. Rooth (1985)).

(13) a. MARY always said hi to John.
 b. Mary always said hi to JOHN.

If someone other than Mary said hi to John, (13a) is false but (13b) may be true. On the other hand, if Mary greeted someone other than John, (13a) may be true but (13b) is false. Herburger proposes that Q-adverbs such as *always* move via a process of Q-raising and focal mapping applies to the resultant structure. (13a, b) are represented in (14a, b) respectively.

(14) a. [Always [said hi to John]] [Mary said hi to John]
 b. [Always [Mary said hi]] [Mary said hi to John]

In (14a), *always* quantifies over events of greeting John, while in (14b) it quantifies over events of Mary's greeting. (14a, b) are mapped to the "structured Davidsonian decomposition," as represented in (15a, b).

(15) a. [all e: C(e) & Say-hi(e) & Past(e) & To(e, john)] (Agent(e, mary) & Say-hi(e) & Past(e) & To(e, john))
'All (relevant) events of saying hi to John had Mary as their agent.'
b. [all e: C(e) & Say-hi(e) &Past(e) & Agent(e, mary)] (To(e, john) & Say-hi(e) & Past(e) & Agent(e, mary))
'All (relevant) events of Mary's saying hi were directed to John.'

Herburger proposes that universal quantifiers have existential force and have the interpretation given in (16).

(16) [all e: F(e)] G(e) iff F≠{}&F⊆G

(16) states that "a universal quantification over events is true when it is the case that the restriction is not empty and every event that is an element of the restriction is also an element of the scope" (Herburger (2000:106)). This ensures that in (15a) the set of past events involving saying hi to John is not empty and that all its members are also members of the set of events where Mary said hi to John.

5.4.2 Quantificational Variability

For a precise understanding of how Herburger's theory of focus works for adverbs of quantification, the following will briefly review the Kamp-Heim theory and compare it with Herburger's analysis. The main linguistic motivation for the Kamp-Heim approach to adverbs of quantification comes from the fact that classical logic fails to account for the truth conditions of so-called donkey sentences. For example, the most straightforward translation of (17a) into classical logic would be as in (17b).

(17) a. If Pedro owns a donkey, he beats it.
   b. (∃x (donkey (x) & own (Pedro, x)) ⟶ beat (he, x))

This treats the indefinite as an existential quantifier, which is the standard in classical logic. (17b), however, fails to capture the intuitive interpretation of (17a). A more appropriate semantic interpretation of (17a) would be (18).[4]

(18) ∀x (donkey (x) & own (Pedro, x) ⟶ beat (Pedro, x))

(18) shows that the indefinite that appears inside the antecedent clause in (17a) gets interpreted as a wide scope universal quantifier. A question then arises as to why indefinites sometimes must be existential quantifiers and at other times need to be analyzed as universal quantifiers.

Adverbs of quantification such as *always* and *rarely* introduce another problem:

(19) a. If a man owns a donkey, he always beats it.
   b. Sometimes if a man owns a donkey, he beats it.
   c. If a man owns a donkey, he rarely beats it.

The quantificational force of the indefinite changes from an existential quantifier to different quantifiers depending on its environment. It is interpreted as a universal quantifier when used with the Q-adverb *always*, and becomes an existential quantifier when the sentence contains an existential adverb such as *sometimes*. The quantificational force of the indefinite varies depending on what Q-adverbs happen to be around. If we assume that the indefinite is an existential quantifier, how do we account for this change in quantificational force? Various

---

[4] Given the c-command requirement for variable binding, the LF representation that corresponds to (17b) is not well formed, since the existential quantifier in the antecedent clause fails to bind the pronoun *it*, which is translated as a variable. In (18), on the other hand, the universal quantifier has scope over the consequent clause and is able to bind the occurrence of x corresponding to the pronoun *it*.

versions of Discourse Representation Theory (DRT) including the Kamp-Heim approach addressed these problems and the basic proposals shared by DRT include the following (cf. Kamp 1981, Heim 1982, Kadmon 1987, 1990, Diesing 1992, and many others).

(i) Both definites and indefinites are treated as variables rather than quantifiers. Definite NPs (including pronouns) are assumed to introduce old variables, whereas indefinites introduce new variables.
(ii) Quantificational adverbs are unselective quantifiers binding all the variables in their scope that are not bound by other quantifiers.
(iii) Universal quantification and conditionals introduce an implicit unselective universal quantifier having scope over the antecedent and the consequent. There is an implicit unselective existential quantifier (existential closure) having scope over the consequent.

Herburger's neo-Davidsonian analysis differs radically from the DRT approach in the following main points.

(i) Both definites and indefinites are genuine quantifiers and do not introduce free variables.
(ii) Quantificational adverbs are selective quantifiers over events.
(iii) There is no default existential generalization of free variables.

Herburger claims that quantificational determiners, frequency adverbs and the hidden operator in conditions are selective in that they just bind one variable each, and that indefinites are treated as existential quantifiers. How the indefinite captures quantificational variability is illustrated by the following example (Herburger 2000:75).

(20) a. A CLAUSTROPHOBIC usually avoids an elevator.

b. [most e: C(e) & Avoid (e) & [an x: Elevator(x)] Theme (e,x)] [a y: Claustrophobic (y)] (Experiencer (e,y) & Avoid (e) & [an x: Elevator (x)]Theme (e,x))
'Most (relevant) events of avoiding an elevator are events of a claustrophobic's avoiding the elevator.'

Herburger proposes that (20a) is translated into the structured Davidsonian decomposition in (20b); namely, focus reshapes the quantificational structure of the Q-adverb, and as a result, the non-focused indefinite *an elevator* appears in its restriction.[5] The interpretation of the indefinite in the restriction varies with the assignments to the event variable *e* of the Q-adverb. (20) means that "in most events *e* of an elevator's being avoided, the one avoiding it is a claustrophobic." It follows that the non-focused indefinite gives rise to quantificational variability.

5.5 Analysis

In the above sections, I have presented an overview of the semantic theory of focus developed by Herburger (2000), in particular highlighting her claim that focus restructures quantificational structure in that the non-focused material in the scope of a quantifier also contributes to its restriction. In this section, I will argue that Herburger's semantic approach does not always give correct interpretations of an indefinite in a conditional clause. My argument is given in relation to the two substantive problems that DRT theory runs into; namely, proportion problems and uniqueness, as addressed by Kadmon (1987, 1990).

---

[5] In the translation given in (20b), the non-focused indefinite *an elevator* occurs twice, once in the restriction and once in the scope of the Q-adverb. Assuming with Larson and Segal (1995) that theta-roles have to be assigned exhaustively, Herburger claims that the same elevator is picked up in both instances.

5.5.1 Proportion Problems

Kadmon (1987, 1990) observes that a conditional with two indefinites as in (21) technically allows multiple interpretations.

(21) Mostly, if a woman owns a dog, she is rich.

One reading is obtained by counting woman-dog pairs (symmetric reading), and the other by counting dog-owning women (asymmetric reading). Suppose that among ten women, one woman who owns 50 dogs is rich, but the other nine women who own exactly one dog are poor. In this scenario (21) is true on the symmetric reading since there are 59 different woman-dog pairs and in most of those pairs the woman is rich. (21), however, is false under the asymmetric reading which is obtained by counting dog-owning women. On this reading, it does not matter how many dogs are owned by a single woman. The sentence is false because there are ten dog-owning women and only one of them is rich. A question then arises as to which of the indefinites is most likely to end up in the restriction of the quantifier. Bauerle and Egli (1985) (cited in Kadmon (1987, 1990)) propose that the Q-adverb quantifies over the indefinite in the antecedent that is linked to the pronoun in the consequent. That is, unless a suitable contextual story is added, *mostly* in (21) quantifies over dog-owning women because the pronoun *she* in the consequent is linked to *a woman* in the antecedent.

Under Herburger's account, the interpretation of the conditionals with two indefinites depends on which of the indefinites is focused. Herburger (2000:78) claims that the indefinite linked with the pronoun in the consequent may not be focused, as exemplified by (22a, b).

(22) a. Mostly, if a woman owns A DOG, she is rich.
     b. #Mostly, if A WOMAN owns a dog, she is rich.

The Davidsonian decomposition of the *if*-clause that Herburger proposes looks like (23), where the Q-adverb *mostly* behaves as if it directly quantified over the events quantified by the conditional operator (∀e').

(23) [most e: C(e) & [∀e': C(e') & One-to-one (e, e') & Own (e') & [an x: Woman (x)] Agent (e', x)][a y: Dog(y)] Theme (e', y)] (Rich(e) & Theme (e, she))

The direct interpretation of (23) would be "most events e where every event e' of a woman's owning that corresponds one-to-one to e is an event involving a dog are such that the woman in e is rich.[6] According to Herburger, the quantificational variability is captured by the indefinite interpreted in the restriction of the conditional operator (∀e'). Given that focus reshapes the quantificational structure of the conditional, (23) has only an asymmetric reading where we are counting dog-owning women, which may in fact give a correct interpretation.

5.5.2 Problems with Herburger's Analysis

Herburger assumes with Heim (1990) that although the pronoun in the consequent tends to be linked with the non-focused indefinite in the antecedent, the context makes it possible for the pronoun to be anaphoric on a focused phrase. This is illustrated in (24), as given originally by Heim (1990).

(24) Donkeys that belong to peddlers generally are in miserable shape, whereas those that belong to farmers mostly have a comfortable life. The reason is that if A FARMER owns a donkey, he is usually rich (and uses tractors and other modern equipment for the hard work on his farm).

Under Herburger's approach, there is only one reading available in (24), namely, that in which the non-focused indefinite that appears in the restriction

---

[6] In (23), the woman in e is not related to the woman in e'. Under Herburger's analysis, since the indefinite is treated as an existential quantifier, the anaphoric pronoun in the consequent cannot be treated as a bound variable. Herburger, however, left open the question of how to treat the existential binding of pronouns.

captures quantificational variability. However, as Heim (1990) pointed out, a preference for one reading over others is a mere tendency that can be overridden by other pragmatic factors (see also Kadmon (1987)).[7] Contrary to what Herburger assumes, (24) could have other readings, such as the reading that Bauerle and Egli (1985) predict, where the Q-adverb quantifies over farmers linked to the pronoun in the consequent clause. Note that even under the given context, we cannot ignore the farmers who own multiple donkeys to get the right interpretation. Suppose one farmer who owns 200 donkeys is rich, but 50 other farmers who own exactly one donkey are poor. Herburger's neo-Davidsonian approach predicts that (24) is true, since 200 out of 250 donkeys are owned by rich farmers. In this scenario, however, (24) can be false by counting donkey-owning farmers rather than donkeys owned by farmers. It seems that how the domain of quantification is delimited depends heavily on pragmatic factors and not merely on focus structure. The same observation holds of (25).

(25) Drummers mostly live in crowded dormitories. But if a drummer lives in an APARTMENT COMPLEX, it is usually half empty.

Under Herburger's analysis, only the non-focused indefinite shows quantificational variability. (25) is false under the context where 200 out of 299 drummers who live in apartment complexes live in apartment complexes that are fully occupied. (25), however, can be read as having a so-called "uniqueness implication" in the sense of Kadmon (1987:197); if a drummer lives in an apartment complex, there is a "unique" apartment complex per drummer. If this is so, the sentence has the same truth condition as a symmetric constral obtained by counting drummer-apartment pairs, rather than counting drummers living in an apartment complex. As for the asymmetric reading, whether we count the drummers or the apartment complexes is a context dependent affair.

---

[7] Heim (1990), in fact, proposes that a semantic theory should not be too successful in predicting the interpretation of the indefinite in multi-case conditionals.

Suppose that the context is given in such a way that we count the apartment complexes. In such a case, if 20 drummers live in one apartment complex that is fully occupied, and exactly one drummer lives in each of 10 other apartment complexes that are half empty, (25) is intuitively true. In summary, although focusing may have some effect on the interpretation of the indefinite, multi-case conditionals with two indefinites allow multiple interpretations regardless of which of the indefinites is focused. The absence of the backgrounded focal entailment inside the *if*-clause illustrated by example (12a) and the proportion problem just discussed above suggest that focus does not affect the quantification structure of a conditional operator.

5.6 Syntactic Account

The aim of this section is to explore a syntactic account for how focus affects quantificational structure. In this section, I will discuss cases in which the "Herburger-style" focus affected reading never arises, and claim that the syntax plays a crucial role in determining the presence or absence of a focus-affected reading. Following Diesing's (1992) basic insight, I argue that a focused phrase moves covertly to the domain of CP and that covert focus movement allows for a straightforward mapping into the "Herburger-style" focus-affected reading.

5.6.1 Diesing's Mapping Hypothesis

Before getting to my syntactic account, I give here a brief explanation of the Mapping Hypothesis proposed by Diesing (1992), which states that there is a direct link between semantic representations and syntactic representations. Following the Kamp-Heim approach, Diesing proposes that a tripartite logical structure consisting of a quantifier, a restrictive clause and the nuclear scope is derived directly from S-structure, as expressed by the Mapping Hypothesis in (26).

(26) Mapping Hypothesis (Diesing 1992:10)
Material from VP is mapped into the nuclear scope.
Material from IP is mapped into a restrictive clause.

The Mapping Hypothesis accounts for the difference in the interpretation of bare plurals with stage and individual level predicates, as illustrated in (27a, b).

(27) a. Blowfish are available.
b. Blowfish are poisonous.

Diesing claims that the subject of the stage level predicate in (27a) is base-generated in Spec(VP), which is mapped into the nuclear scope, whereas the subject of the individual level predicate is base-generated in Spec(IP), and is mapped into the restrictive clause. (27a, b) are represented in (28a, b) respectively.

(28) a. $\exists_x$ x is blowfish & x is available.
b. Gen_x[x is blowfish] x is poisonous

(28a) involves only scope and no restriction is formed, whereas (28b) illustrates a tripartite logical structure consisting of the Gen-operator, the restrictive clause and the nuclear scope. Diesing (1992:49) observes that focus contributes to the interpretation of bare plurals, suggesting that focused material is mapped into the nuclear scope in its logical representation. This is illustrated by the contrast given in (29a, b).

(29) a. I only said that [F BLOWFISH are available].
b. *I only said that [F BLOWFISH are poisonous].

When the subject of the stage level predicate is focused, it allows a wide focus reading in which focus projects to the entire sentence. (29a) can be interpreted as 'the only thing I said was that blowfish are available, and I did not say anything else'. When the subject of an individual level predicate is focused, in contrast, focus does not go beyond the NP. (29b) is not acceptable with the projected wide focus reading. What follows is that focus can project from Spec(VP), but not from Spec(IP). Herburger, however, argues against the Mapping Hypothesis that states that an element inside a VP is automatically mapped to the adverb's nuclear scope. She observes that in examples (30a, b), the non-focused material inside the VP is mapped not to the scope of the Q-adverb, but to its restriction at the logical representation.

(30) a. David rarely reads THE NEWSPAPER.
    b. DAVID rarely reads the newspaper.

Since Diesing's analysis of focus mainly concerns a wide focus that is bound by existential closure, how the Mapping Hypothesis works for (30a, b) is entirely left open. In the following sections, I will argue that while the projected focus in (29a) is interpreted inside the VP, as proposed by Diesing, the unprojected narrow focus as in (29b) and (30a, b) involves covert focus movement that results in the restructuring of the quantificational structure of focus sensitive operators.

5.6.2 A Phase-Based Minimalist Approach

There has been a long-standing theoretical question whether focused materials are interpreted *in-situ* or they involve LF movement. A well-known empirical argument for the *in-situ* analysis of focus, as proposed by Herburger, is that focus is insensitive to syntactic island conditions such as Subjacency:

(31)   John only knows a boy who lives in TOKYO.

Despite the fact that *only* and the associated focused phrase are non-local in examples like (31), it will be shown that there is substantial evidence that the "Herburger-style" focus affected reading arises only as a result of covert focus movement.

The basic syntactic framework I will be assuming in this chapter is that of the phase-based minimalist approach recently developed by Chomsky (2001a, 2001b). Two major components that differ crucially from the earlier versions of Chomsky's minimalist approach are as follows. First, Spell-out is taken to apply cyclically at the strong phase level, which is identified as vP (light verb phrase) and CP. The cyclic Spell-out system lends itself to the conclusion that three components: narrow syntax (NS), LF and PF, proceed cyclically in parallel. Subjacency reduces to the so-called Phase Impenetrability Condition (PIC) that reduces the search domain for operations:

(32) The Phase Impenetrability Condition
In phase α with head H, the domain of H is not accessible to operations outside α, only H and its edge are accessible to such operations.

(Chomsky 2001a:13)

Due to PIC, the phonological components do not look into the earlier stages. For illustrative purposes, consider (33).

(33) [$_{CP}$...[$_{vP}$ α[$_v$ [VP...]]]]

VP is spelled-out at the level of vP. The status of the edge of vP, α and v, is determined at the next strong phase CP. This means that the edge of vP is accessible to operations outside vP and hence movement must uniformly proceed through the edge of the phase. The second component of the phase-based minimalist assumption that is crucial to the thesis of this chapter concerns the assumption that the edge of the strong phase requires some particular interpretive mechanism at the conceptual-intentional (C-I) interface.

Given that the application of movement is motivated by non-theta theoretic C-I interface conditions, Chomsky (2001b) introduces the feature called OCC (meaning "I must be an occurrence of some β"), which has the following characteristics:

"OCC should be available only when necessary: that is, when it contributes to an outcome at SEM that is not otherwise expressible. [A head] H has OCC only if it yields new scopal or discourse-related properties (or if required for other reasons). If H has OCC, then the new interpretive options are established if OCC is checked by internal Move; it is only necessary that the cyclic derivation D can continue so that they are ultimately satisfied with convergence of D. Informally, we can think of OCC as having the "function" of providing new interpretations."   (Chomsky 2001b:11)

Scope of *wh*-phrases, for example, has a long distance property. Assuming that a subject is generated in Spec(vP), the PIC forces the *wh*-phrase to move through the outer edge of vP successive cyclically. Note importantly that this outer edge position is completely optional. The feature OCC not only makes this position available for *wh*-movement, but also makes each step of *wh*-movement satisfy C-I interface conditions.

5.6.3 Covert Focus Movement

Under Chomsky's minimalist framework, a light verb phrase vP contains multiple Specs and the outer Spec serves as an intermediate landing site for *wh*-movement. I argued in the previous chapters that a *wh*-phrase moves to CP through a clause internal position, but that this position projects its own X-bar schema; namely, a head Foc^0 has a specifier position and a VP as its complement. For present purposes, I assume that the outer edge of vP has independent categorial status, corresponding to FocP under my account. FocP serves as a strong phase, and as discussed in Chapter 4, its existence is optional and available whenever a clause contains a focus constituent. Covert focus movement, then, directly feeds into semantic structure at the FocP and CP phases.[8] I propose that focal mapping in the sense of Herburger (2000) is

---

[8] Following the basic minimalist conception, a computational system has no access to discourse-related interpretations. It follows that covert focus movement should not be described as driven by the semantic feature of a focused element. The focus-affected reading is then understood as one of the properties of the resulting configuration.

taken to be the interface condition that applies at the phase level. The bipartite semantic structure is compositionally derived from the structure provided by the syntax, as illustrated in (34a-d).

(34) a. [$_{VP}$ John loves MARY]   Base structure
    b. [$_{FocP}$ MARY [$_{VP}$ John loves t]]   Focus movement
    c. [$_{CP}$ MARY [$_{FocP}$ t [$_{VP}$ John loves t]]]
    d. [$_{VP}$ John loves][$_{CP}$ MARY John loves]   Bipartite structure

Given that focus is licensed at the edge of the phase, the focused phrase MARY in (34a) moves covertly to FocP, leaving behind a trace. For present purposes, it is assumed that at the conceptual-intentional (C-I) interface, only one member of the chain is interpreted and all other members actually delete (cf. Hornstein 1999). After spelling out the VP, the VP in (34b) is mapped into the semantic restriction.[9] Crucially, since the element in FocP is interpreted at CP, a focused phrase moves to CP as in (34c), which is mapped into the scope of focus. (Chomsky (2001) stipulates that interpretation takes place uniformly at the next higher phase. See Chomsky (2001:13) for detailed discussion.) The bipartite semantic structure compositionally constructed as in (34d) then is translated into the structured Davidsonian decomposition:

(35)   [∃e: C(e) & love (e) & Experiencer (e, john)] (Theme (e, mary) & Experiencer (e, john) & love (e))

The interpretation of (35) states that some relevant event of John's loving is such that it is an event of John's loving and its theme is Mary. My proposed analysis, however, differs from Herburger's in that it assumes that there are

---

[9] The assumption that verbs are fully inflected in the lexicon allows tense information along with the VP to be mapped into the restriction of the event quantifier. Note that under Diesing's Mapping Hypothesis, a restrictive clause and the nuclear scope correspond to IP and VP respectively. I propose that focus has the reversed effect in that VP is mapped into the semantic restriction.

two types of focus. A wide focus reading does not involve covert movement, and as a result, (36) is ambiguous between the "Diesing-style" reading and the "Herburger-style" reading.

(36)   CHILDREN are playing.

The "Diesing-style" reading simply asserts that there is an event where CHILDREN are playing (i.e. wide focus), and the "Herburger-style" reading states that some relevant event of playing is an event where CHILDREN are playing. The former involves no covert focus movement and hence no restriction is formed, whereas the latter involves covert focus movement, forming the restriction of the event quantifier. I propose that covert focus movement is treated as an optional movement, and that the "Herburger-style" focus-affected reading is understood as one of the properties of the resulting configuration.

The optionality of covert focus movement is motivated on both theoretical and empirical grounds. On theoretical grounds, focus movement is driven by the optional feature [+Focus] available only when a clause contains a focused constituent. On empirical grounds, the optionality of focus movement provides an account for why backgrounded focal entailments are suspended in embedded clauses like (37) (cf. (12a)).

(37)   If HILLARY trusts Bill, all is well.

Suppose that the conditional operator is licensed at CP. Then the embedded CP is not available for the focused phrase, and as a result, the focused phrase ends up staying *in-situ* and does not form a bipartite semantic structure.[10] Note

---

[10] I assume that in a multiple Spec construction, only non-distinct XPs can be licensed at the edge of a phase. The view that the conditional operator is licensed at the edge of the phase CP is supported by the fact that subject-Aux inversion is possible when *if* is not present:
(i)   a.   If John had done that, he would be happy.
      b.   Had John done that, he would be happy.

further that focus does not go beyond the *if*-clause and affect the quantificational structure of the matrix clause. The reason why focus cannot be raised out of the *if*-clause is accounted for by the Minimal Link Condition (MLC), as discussed in details in Chapter 2.

(38) Minimal Link Condition (MLC) (Chomsky 1995:311)
K attracts α only if there is no β, β closer to K than α, such that K attracts β.

The MLC prohibits establishment of a checking relation between the matrix Comp and the focused phrase, in the presence of the conditional operator. In other words, the MLC, which is assumed to be part of the definition of Move, is applicable to covert focus movement as well. In Chapter 2, I have presented a number of arguments for the view that covert *wh*-movement is sensitive to the MLC, the issue of which will be further discussed in 5.6.4.

5.6.4 Two Kinds of Determiners

The idea that there are two kinds of focus, one with quantificational force and the other without quantificational force, is strongly supported by the well-known descriptive observation concerning two types of determiners, which Milsark (1974) calls strong and weak. Milsark observes that strong determiners cannot appear in *there*-insertion contexts (the so-called "definiteness effect"), while weak determiners can appear in *there*-insertion contexts. This is illustrated in (39a, b).

(39) a. *There is (are) every/each/all child(ren) in the garden.
  b. There are some/three/many/few/no children in the garden.

Milsark further indicates that strong determiners carry existential presuppositions:

(40) a. Every child baked banana pie.
   b. Most children ate banana pie.

Both the sentences in (40a, b) carry a presupposition that children must in fact exist. Weak determiners, on the other hand, are ambiguous. The non-presuppositional reading, which Milsark calls a cardinal reading, simply asserts the existence of entities:

(41) a. There are some children in the garden.
   b. Some children are in the garden; the others are in the kitchen.

(41a) favors the non-presuppositional reading; the sentence simply asserts the existence of children in the garden. If children turn out not to exist, the sentence is false. (40b) favors the presuppositional reading, and can be paraphrased as a partitive: some of the children. With the presuppositional reading, the absence of children does not make the sentence false, but rather its truth-value will be undefined. Given Milsark's classification of the two types of determiners, Herburger observes that the weak determiners, but not the strong determiners, allow focus-affected readings.[11] This is exemplified by (42a, b).

(42) a. Some/Few/Many/No/students from NEW YORK applied.
   b. Every/All/Each students from NEW YORK applied.

(42a) allows a focus affected interpretation, stating that some/few/many/no students who applied were from New York. The focus-affected reading, however, is impossible in (42b). Namely, (42b) cannot be paraphrased as every/all/each student who applied was from New York. Under Herburger's analysis, weak determiners (some, few, etc.) behave like adverbial quantifiers in how

---

[11] Herburger does not appeal to the presuppositional treatment of the quantificational determiners. Under Herburger's analysis, the existence of children in (40) and (41) is entailed, rather than presupposed. If children do not exist, the sentences are not valueless, but they are simply false.

they find their restrictions. Weak determiners take scope through Q-raising, as illustrated in (43).

(43) D_i [$_{DP}$ t_i NP] YP

Focus reshapes the quantificational structure after Q-raising takes place. (42a) becomes (44a) after Q-raising, and then becomes (44b) after focal mapping.

(44) a. [Some [student from NEW YORK applied]]   [Q-raising]
     b. [[Some [student applied]] [student from NEW YORK applied]]
                                                   [Focal mapping]

To account for the absence of the focus-affected reading in (42b), Herburger suggests that strong determiners do not undergo Q-raising. Note that focal mapping applies only after Q is raised to a position from which it c-commands both the focus and the rest of the non-focused material. It follows that if Q-raising does not take place, the focus-affected reading is not available. Although the Q-raising analysis seems to work for distinguishing between weak and strong determiners, Herburger provides no principled independent explanation for why weak determiners, but not strong determiners, undergo Q-raising. Without appeal to the Q-raising analysis, I will argue that the difference between (42a) and (42b) is attributable to the MLC.

5.6.5 Intervention Effects

It is well known that *wh*-movement out of an NP depends on the semantic properties of the NP, in particular, it is sensitive to a Specificity condition (cf. Fiengo and Higginbotham 1981), as illustrated in (45a, b).

(45) a. Who did you see a picture of ?
     b. *Who did you see the picture of?

The *wh*-word can move out of an indefinite NP, but not out of a definite NP.

5 Focus Movement and Semantic Interpretation   163

Diesing (1992) suggests that the contrast given in (45a, b) can be assimilated to Milsark's characterization of two kinds of determiners: weak determiners in (46) and strong determiners in (47).

(46) a. Who did you see a picture of?
   b. Who did you see many pictures of?
   c. Who did you see several pictures of?
   d. Who did you see some pictures of?

(47) a.*?Who did you see the picture of?
   b.*?Who did you see every picture of?
   c.*?Who did you see most pictures of?
   d.*?Who did you see each picture of?   (Diesing 1992:97)

Diesing (1992) proposes that strong determiners with existential presuppositions have quantificational force of their own and undergo QR at LF, while non-presuppositional weak determiners have no quantificational force and involve no movement. The contrast given in (46) and (47) is accounted for by the following constraint.

(48)   Presuppositional NP constraint (Diesing 1992:103)
       Extraction cannot take place out of a presuppositional NP.

Diesing argues that there are two kinds of indefinite NPs; indefinites with an existential reading are construed as non-quantificational variables bound by existential closure, whereas indefinites with a presuppositional reading have a quantificational force of their own and undergo QR.[12] Due to the condition in (48), it is predicted that only the former allows *wh*-movement out of the NPs.

---
[12] Diesing has shown that while quantificational indefinites move covertly in English, those in German move overtly to a position immediately above VP. Diesing's (1992) observations concerning indefinites lend support to the existence of a clause internal operator position (For a detailed discussion, see Chapter 2).

This is evidenced by examples (49) and (50).

(49) a. Who do you usually read a book by?
　　 b. Who do you usually play a sonata by?
　　 c. What do you usually buy a picture of?
　　 d. Who do you usually comment on an essay by?
　　 e. What do you usually publish a book about? (ibid.116)

(50) a. *What do you usually like a picture of?
　　 b. *Who do you usually love a sonata by?
　　 c. *What you do usually appreciate a good joke about?
　　 d. *What do you usually hate an article about?
　　 e. *What do you generally detest an opera by? (ibid. 117)

All the predicates in (49) have an indefinite object with an existential reading and extraction out of the NPs is possible. Experiencer predicates in (50), however, allow only a presuppositional reading of their object NPs and extraction out of the NPs is not possible. Under the phase-based minimalist framework, scopal properties of quantifiers are assigned at the edge of the phase, and the constraint (48) may be reformulated in (51).

(51) Presuppositional NP constraint (Revised)
　　 Extraction cannot take place out of an NP that must itself be interpreted at the edge of a phase.

It is clear that the constraint (51) is reducible to the MLC, as stated in (38). Suppose that covert movement behaves exactly like overt *wh*-movement with respect to the MLC. It is predicted that focus *in-situ* may have the same distributional similarity. Consider (52) and (53).

(52) a. I usually read a book by CHOMSKY.
   b. I usually play a sonata by DITTERSDORF.
   c. I usually buy a picture of THE CHIRICAHUAS.
   d. I usually comment on an essay by GEORGE WILL.
   e. I usually publish a book on CHOMSKY.

(53) a. I usually like a picture of MANATEES.
   b. I usually love a sonata by DITTERSDORF.
   c. I usually appreciate a joke about VIOLISTS.
   d. I usually hate an article about CARPENTER ANTS.
   e. I usually detest an opera by MOZART.

Unlike *wh*-movement, none of these sentences are excluded in the syntax, and yet the "Herburger-style" focus-affected reading is possible in (52), but not possible in (53). Example (52a), for instance, can mean that most events of my reading a book are events of my reading a book by Chomsky (here usually "associates" with CHOMSKY). (53a), however, cannot mean that most events of my liking a picture are events of my liking a picture of manatees. The unavailability of the "Herburger-style" focus-affected reading is not due to the fact that the predicate associated with the indefinite is stative since Herburger makes no distinction between episodic and stative predicates with respect to the notion of the event. (53a) only means that whenever I see a picture of manatees, I like it. In other words, the Q-adverb is restricted by the object NP and the focused phrase is interpreted inside the NP, which is automatically mapped into Q's restriction. This supports the view that the presuppositional indefinite NP moves to the edge of the phase and a focused phrase inside the NP may not move out of the NP in violation of the MLC. Now consider (54a, b).

(54) a. Some/Few/Many students from NEW YORK are intelligent.
   b. Most students from NEW YORK are intelligent.

Although both (54a, b) are acceptable sentences, neither allows the focus-affected reading; these sentences cannot mean some/few/many/most intelligent students are from NEW YORK. The absence of the focus-affected reading in (54a, b) has to do with the fact that the focused phrases appear in the subject position of an individual-level predicate. Recall that under the Mapping Hypothesis, Diesing (1988, 1992) proposes that the subject of the individual-level predicate is base-generated in Spec(IP), which is mapped into the restrictive clause, and that the variable introduced in the restrictive clause is bound by a default generic operator Gen. Suppose that the scopal properties of Gen are assigned at the edge of the phase. The absence of the focus-affected reading in (54a, b) is then accounted for straightforwardly by the MLC.

To summarize, it is argued that focus undergoes covert movement and that focus movement behaves exactly like *wh*-movement in that it is subject to the MLC. Covert focus movement, however, differs from *wh*-movement in that it is an optional movement that takes place only if it has a semantic effect on the outcome.

5.7 Concluding Remarks

Diesing has argued for a direct link between syntactic representations and semantic representations within the framework of generative grammar. Herburger's framework provides a non-transformational, compositional dynamic formalism for deducing the semantic representations. Despite their apparent radical distinctness, this chapter has explored an attempt to mediate the two theories, showing that covert focus movement allows for a straightforward mapping into "Herburger-style" focus interpretations involving structured Davidsonian decomposition.

I have adopted two major syntactic components that are central to the phase-based minimalist framework. The first concerns the notion of cyclic Spell-out whereby syntactic structure feeds into semantic structure at the strong phase level. The system lends itself naturally to the conclusion that LF and PF components are accessible in a dynamic way. The second concerns the kind of feature, referred to as OCC, which is an optional feature available only when it contributes to new scopal or discourse-related interpretations. I have suggested that the "Herburger-style" focus-affected reading results from checking of OCC by internal Merge that triggers covert focus movement. This provides a straightforward syntactic account for the conditions under which focus gives rise to "backgrounded focal entailments" in the sense of Herburger.

Old Japanese Texts

Primary Sources

Manyoshu, Nakanishi Susumu, Koudansha Bunko, Tokyo (1980 (reprinted in 2002)).

Manyoshu, Nihon Koten Bungaku Taikei, 4-7, Iwanami Shoten, Tokyo (1957-1962).

The Man'yo-Shu, Teruo Suga, Kanda University of International Studies, Makuhari, (1991).

Konkomyou Saisho Okyou: Koten no Kokugogakuteki Kenkyu, Kasuga Masaji, Bensei Sha (1969)

Electronic Texts

Japanese Text Initiative Electronic Text Center, University of Virginia Library (http://etext.lib.virginia.edu/japanese/jti.texts.euc.html)

National Institute of Japanese Literature (http://www.nijl.ac.jp/contents/d_library/index.html)

Yoshimura Makoto (http://yoshi01.kokugo.edu.yamaguchi-u.ac.jp/manyou/manyou.html)

References

Adachi, Ryuuichi (1992) 'Kokugo Koubunshi no Ichisokumen: Shukaku Muhyouji Koubun kara Shukaku Hyouji Koubun-e', In Chikao Inoue and Yoichiro Yamauchi (eds), *Kodaigo no Kouzou to Tenkai*, pp.1-23, Izumi Shoin, Osaka.

Aoun, Joseph and Audrey Li (1993) *Syntax of Scope*, MIT Press, Cambridge, MA.

Aoun, Joseph, Norbert Hornstein and Dominique Sportiche (1981) 'Some Aspects of Wide Scope Quantification', *Journal of Linguistic Research* 1:3, 69-95.

Awobuluyi, Oladele (1992) 'Issues in the Syntax of Standard Yoruba Focus Constructions', *Journal of West African Languages* 22, 71-88

Bach, Emmon (1971) 'Questions', *Linguistic Inquiry* 2, 153-166.

Baker, Lee C (1968) 'Indirect Questions in English', Doctoral Dissertation, University of Illinois, Urbana.

Baker, Mark C (1988) *Incorporation: A Theory of Grammatical Function Changing*, University of Chicago Press, Chicago.

Belletti, Adriana (1990) *Generalized Verb Movement*, Rosenberg and Sellier, Torino.

Belletti, Adriana (1994) 'Verb Positions: Evidence from Italian', In David Lightfoot and Norbert Hornstein (eds.), *Verb Movement*, pp. 19-40, Cambridge University Press, Cambridge.

Bobaljik, Jonathan David (1994) 'What Does Adjacency Do?', *The Morphology-Syntax Connection, MIT Working Papers in Linguistics* 22, 1-32. MIT, Cambridge, Mass.

Cheng, Lisa (1991) 'On the Typology of *Wh*-Questions', Doctoral Dissertation, MIT, Mass.

Choe, Jae W (1982) 'LF Movement and Pied-piping', *Linguistic Inquiry* 18.

Chomsky, Noam (1977) 'On *Wh*-Movement', In Peter W. Culicover, Thomas Wasow, and Adrian Akamajian (eds.), *Formal Syntax*, Academic Press, New York.

Chomsky, Noam (1981) *Lectures on Government and Binding*, Foris, Dordrecht.

Chomsky, Noam (1986a) *Barriers*, MIT press, Cambridge, Mass.

Chomsky, Noam (1986b) *Knowledge of Language*, Praeger, New York.

Chomsky, Noam (1989) ''Some Notes on Economy of Derivation and Representation', *MIT Working Papers in Linguistics* 10, 43-74.

Chomsky, Noam (1993) 'A Minimalist Program for Linguistic Theory', In Kenneth Hale and Samuel Jay Keyser (eds.), *The View from Building 20*, pp. 1-52, The MIT Press. Cambridge, Mass.

Chomsky, Noam (1995) *The Minimalist Program*, MIT Press, Cambridge, Mass.

Chomsky, Noam (2000) 'Minimalist Inquiries: Framework', In Roger Martin, David Michaels, and Juan Uriagereka (eds.), *Step by Step*, pp. 89-155, MIT Press, Cambridge, Mass.

Chomsky, Noam (2001a) 'Derivation by Phase', In Michael Kenstowicz (ed.), *Ken Hale: A Life in Language*, pp.1-52, MIT Press, Cambridge, Mass.

Chomsky, Noam (2001b) 'Beyond Explanatory Adequacy', In *MIT Occasional Papers in Linguistics* 20, MIT, Cambridge, Mass.

Culicover, Peter (1991) 'Topicalization, Inversion and Complementizers in English', manuscript, The Ohio State University.

den Besten, Hans (1983) 'On the Interaction of Root Transformations and Lexical Deletive Rules', In Werner Abraham (ed.), *On the Formal Syntax of the Westgermania*, pp. 47-131, John Benjamins, Amsterdam.

Déprez, Viviane (1989) 'On the Typology of Syntactic Positions and the Nature of Chains', Doctoral Dissertation, MIT, Cambridge, Mass.

Diesing, Molly (1988) 'Bare Plurals and the Stage/Individual Contrast', In Manfred Krifka (ed.), *Genericity in Natural Language: Proceedings of the 1988 Tübingen Conference*, pp.107-154.

Diesing, Molly (1992) *Indefinites*, MIT Press, Cambridge, Mass.

Enç Mürvet (1991) 'The Semantics of Specificity,' *Linguistic Inquiry* 22, 1-25.

Fiengo, Robert and James Higginbotham (1981) 'Opacity in NP', *Linguistics Analysis* 7, 395-422.

Fischer, Olga (1994) 'Verbal Complementation in Early ME: How Do the Infinitives Fit in?', In Derek Britton (ed.), *English Historical Linguistics*, pp.247-270, John Benjamins, Amsterdam.

Fischer, Olga (1996) 'The Status of *to* in Old English *to*-infinitives: A reply to Kageyama', *Lingua* 99, 107-133.

Fischer, Olga, Ans van Kemenade, Willem Koopman, and Wim van der Wurff (2000) *The Syntax of Early English*, Cambridge University Press, Cambridge.

Fukui, Naoki (1986) *A Theory of Category Projection and Its Application*, Doctoral Dissertation, MIT, Cambridge, Mass. [Revised version published as *Theory of Projection in Syntax*, CSLI Publications, Stanford (1995)]

Fukui, Naoki (1993) 'Parameters and Optinality', *Linguistic Inquiry* 24, 399-420.

Gelderen, Elly van (1993) *The Rise of Functional Categories*, John Benjamins, Amsterdam.

Givón, Talmy (1979) *On Understanding Grammar*, Academic Press, New York.

Grimshaw, Jane, and Armin Mester (1988) 'Light Verbs and Theta-marking,' *Linguistic Inquiry* 19, 205-232.

Hashimoto, Shinkichi (1969) *Jyoshi, Jyodoshi no Kenkyuu*, Iwanami Shoten, Tokyo.

Heim, Irene (1982) 'The Semantics of Definite and Indefinite Noun Phrases', Doctoral Dissertation, University of Massachussets, Amherst.

Heim, Irene (1990) 'E-type Pronouns and Donkey Anaphora', *Linguistics and Philosophy* 13, 137-177.

Herburger, Elena (2000) *What Counts: Focus and Quantification*, MIT Press, Cambridge, Mass.

Higginbotham, James and Robert May (1981) 'Questions, quantifiers and crossing', *The Linguistic Review* 1, 41-80.

Hock, Hans Henrich (1986) *Principles of Historical Linguistics*, Mouton de Gruyter, Amsterdam.

Hock, Hans Henrich (1992) 'Reconstruction and Syntactic Typology: a Plea for a Different Approach', In Garry. W. Davis and Gregory K. Iverson (eds.), *Explanation in Historical Linguistics*, pp.105-121, John Benjamins, Amsterdam.

Hoji, Hajime (1985) 'Logical Form Constraints and Configurational Structures in Japanese', Doctoral Dissertation, University of Washington.

Holmberg, Anders (1986) 'Word Order and Syntactic Features in the Scandinavian Languages and English', Doctoral Dissertation, University of Stockholm.

Holmberg, Anders (1988) 'The Head of S in Scandinavian and English', *McGill Working Papers in Linguistics*, pp. 123-155.

Holmberg, Anders and Christer Platzack (1991) 'On the Role of Inflection in Scandinavian Syntax', In Werner Abraham, Wim Kosmeijer, and Eric Reuland (eds.), *Issues in Germanic Syntax*, pp. 93-118, Mouton de Gruyter, Berlin.

Hornstein, Norbert (1999) 'Minimalism and Quantifier Raising', In Samuel David Epstein and Norbert Hornstein (eds.), *Working Minimalism*, pp.45-75, MIT Press, Cambridge, Mass.

Horstein, Norbert and Amy Weinberg (1990) 'The Necessity of LF', *The Linguistic Review* 7, 129-167.

Horvath, Julia (1986) *FOCUS in the Theory of Grammar and the Syntax of Hungarian*, Foris, Dordrecht.

Huang, C-T, James (1982) 'Logical Relations in Chinese and the Theory of Grammar', Doctoral Dissertation, MIT, Cambridge, Mass.

Kadmon, Nirit (1987) 'On Unique and Non-unique Reference and Asymmetric Quantification', Doctoral Dissertation, University of Massachusetts, Amherst.

Kadmon, Nirit (1990) 'Uniqueness', *Linguistics and Philosophy* 13, 273-324.

Kageyama, Taro (1992) 'AGR in Old English *to*-infinitives', *Lingua* 88, 91-128.

Kamp, Hans (1981) 'A Theory of Truth and Semantic Representation', In Jeroen Groenendijk, Theo Janssen, and Martin Stokhof (eds.), *Formal Methods in the Study of Language*, pp.277-321, Mathematical Centre, Amsterdam.

Kato, Yasuhiko (2002) 'Negation in Classical Japanese: A Preliminary Survey', *Sophia Linguistica* 49, 99-119.

Kayne, Richard (1991) 'Romance Clitics, Verb Movement, and PRO', *Linguistic Inquiry* 22, 647-686.

Kayne, Richard (1994) *The Antisymmetry of Syntax*, MIT Press, Cambridge, Mass.

Kemenade, Ans van (1987) *Syntactic Case and Morphological Case in the History of English*, Foris, Dordrecht.

Kemenade, Ans van (1993) 'The History of English Modals: A Reanalysis', *Folia Linguistica Historica* 13, 143-166.

Kim, Soo Won (1989) 'Wh-phrases in Korean and Japanese are QPs', *MIT working papers in Linguistics* 11, 119-138, MIT, Cambridge, Mass.

Kim, Soo Won (1990) 'Chain Scope and Quantificational Structure', Doctoral Dissertation, Brandeis University, Waltham.

Kiparsky, Paul (1995) 'Indo-European Origins of Germanic syntax', In Adrian Battye and Ian Roberts (eds.), *Clause Structure and Language Change*, pp.140-169, Oxford University Press, Oxford.

Kishimoto, Hideki (1991) 'On the Nature of Quantificational Expressions and Their Logical Form', Doctoral Dissertation, Kobe University, Kobe.

Kiss, Katalin (1981) 'Structural Relations in Hungarian: A Free Word Order Languages', *Linguistic Inquiry* 12, 185-213.

Kiss, Katalin (1995) *Discourse Configurational Languages*, Oxford University Press, Oxford.

Koji, Kazuteru (1988) *Manyoshu Joshi no Kenkyu*, Kasama Shoin. Tokyo.

Koji, Kazuteru (1980) *Manyoshu Jodoshi no Kenkyu*, Meiji Shoin, Tokyo.

Konoshima, Masatoshi (1973) *Kokugo Joshi No Kenkyuu*, Oofuusha, Tokyo.

Koopman, Hilda (1984) *The Syntax of Verbs: From Verb Movement Rules in the Kru Languages to Universal Grammar*, Foris, Dordrecht.

Koster, Jan (1975) 'Dutch as an SOV Language', *Linguistic Analysis* 1, 111-136.

Krifka, Manfred (1988) 'The Relational Theory of Genericity', In Manfred Krifka (ed.), *Genericity in Natural Language: Proceedings of the 1988 Tübingen Conference*, pp. 285-312.

Krifka, Manfred (1995) 'Focus and the Interpretation of Generic Sentences', In Gregory Carlson and Francis Jeffry Pelletier (eds.), *The GenericBook*, pp. 238-264, University of Chicago Press, Chicago.

Kuno, Susumu (1973) *The Structure of the Japanese Language*, MIT Press, Cambridge, Mass.

Kuroda, Shigeyuki (1988) 'Whether We Agree or Not: A Comparative Syntax of English and Japanese', *Lingvisticæ Investigationes* 12,1-47.

Kuroda, Shigeyuki (1992) *Japanese Syntax and Semantics*, Kluwer Academic Publishers, Dordrecht.

Kuwabara, Kazuki (2001) 'The Focus of the Questions and the Null Copular Constructions', In Kazuko Inoue (ed.), *Report (5): Researching and Verifying an Advanced Theory of Human Language*, Kanda University of International Studies, Makuhari.

Laka, Itziar (1990) 'Negation in Syntax: On the nature of Functional Cagetories and Projections', Doctoral Dissertation, MIT, Cambridge, Mass.

Laka, Itziar (1992) 'Negative Complementizers: Interclausal Licensing of Negative Polarity Items', *NELS* 22, 275-289.

Laka, Itziar (1993) "Unergatives that Assign Ergative, Unaccusatives that Assign Accusative," *MIT Working Papers in Linguistics* 18, 149-172.

Larson, Richard (1988) 'On the Double Object Construction', *Linguistic Inquiry* 19, 335-391.

Larson, Richard, and Gabriel Segal (1995) *Knowledge of Meaning*, MIT Press, Cambridge, Mass.

Lasnik, Howard (1981) 'Restricting the Theory of Transformations', In Hornstein and Lightfoot (eds.), *Explanation in Linguisitics*, Longman, New York.

Lasnik, Howard and Mamoru Saito (1984) 'On the Nature of Proper Government', *Linguistic Inquiry* 15, 235-289.

Lasnik, Howard and Mamoru Saito (1992) *Move α: Conditions on Its Application and Output*, MIT Press, Cambridge, Mass.

Law, Paul (1991) 'Effects of Head-Movement on Theories of Subjacency and Proper Government', Doctoral Dissertation, MIT, Cambridge, Mass.

Law, Paul (1991) 'Verb Movement, Expletive Replacement, and Head Government', *The Linguistic Review* 8, 253-285.

Lehmann, Winfred P. (1974) *Proto-Indo-European Syntax*, University of Texas Press, Austin.

Lehmann, Winfred P. (1976) 'From Topic to Subject in Indo-European', In Li Charles (ed.) *Subject and Topic*, pp. 445-456, Academic Press, New York.

Lewis, David (1975) 'Adverbs of Quantification', In Edward Keenan (ed.), *Formal Semantics of Natural Language*, pp. 3-15, Cambridge University Press, Cambridge, Mass.

Li, Charles N. and Sandra A. Thompson (1976) 'Subject and Topic: A New Typology of Language', In Li Charles (ed.), *Subject and Topic*, pp.457-489. Academic Press, New York.

Li, Yafei (1990) 'Conditions on X^0-movement', Doctoral Dissertation, MIT, Cambridge, Mass.

Lightfoot, David (1979) *Principles of Diachronic Syntax*, Cambridge University Press, Cambridge.

Lightfoot, David (1991) *How to Set Parameters: Arguments from Language Change*, MIT Press, Cambridge, Mass.

Los, Bettelou (1999) *Infinitival Complementation in Old and Middle English*, The Hague, the Netherlands.

Mahajan, Anoop K. (1990) 'The A/A-bar Distinction and Movement Theory', Doctoral Dissertation, MIT, Cambridge, Mass.

McDaniel, Dana (1989) 'Partial and Multiple *Wh*-Movement', *Natural Language and Linguistic Theory* 7, 565-605.

Miller, Gary (2002) *Nonfinite Structures in Theory and Change*, Oxford University Press, Oxford.

Milsark, Gary (1974) *Existential Sentences in English*, Doctoral Dissertation, MIT, Mass. [Published by Garland, New York, 1975]

Miyagawa, Shigeru (1989) *Syntax and Semantics: Structure and Case Marking in Japanese* 22, Academic Press, New York.

Miyagawa, Shigeru (1997) 'Against Optional Scrambling', *Linguistic Inquiry* 28, 1-26.

Miyagawa, Shigeru (2001) 'The EPP, Scrambling, and *Wh-in-situ*', In Michael Kenstowicz (ed.), *Ken Hale: A Life in Language*, pp. 293-338, MIT Press, Cambridge, Mass.

Motohashi, Tatsushi (1989) 'Case Theory and the History of the Japanese Language', Doctoral Dissertation, University of Arizona.

Motohashi, Tatsushi (1995) 'On the Assignment of Genitive *no* in Old Japanese,' *Sophia Linguistica* 10, 190-206.

Motohashi, Tatsushi (2003) 'Nara Period: The Handbook of Historical Japanese Grammar', Manuscript, Sophia University, Tokyo.

Nishigauchi, Taisuke (1986) Quantification in Syntax, Doctoral Dissertation, University of Massachussets, Amherst.

Nishigauchi, Taisuke (1990) *Quantification in the Theory of Grammar*, Kluwer, Dordrecht.

Nomura, Takashi (1993) 'Joudaigo no *no* to *ga* ni tsuite', *Kokugo Kokubun* 62, 1-17.

Nomura, Takashi (1996) '*ga*-Shushikei e', *Kokugo Kokubun* 65, 524-541.

Ogawa, Kunihiko (1976) 'Japanese Interrogatives: A Synchronic and Diachronic Analysis', Doctoral Dissertation, University of California, San Diego.

Ohno, Susumu (1977) 'Shukaku Jyosi *ga* no Seiritsu', *Bungaku* 45, 102-117.

Ohno, Susumu (1993) *Kakarimusubi no Kenkyuu*, Iwanami Shoten, Tokyo.

Ouhalla, Jamal (1990) 'Sentential Negation, Relativized Minimality and the Aspectual Status of Auxiliaries', *The Linguistic Review* 7.183-231.

Parsons, Terence (1990) *Events in the Semantics of English: A Study in Subatomic Semantics*, MIT Press, Cambridge, Mass.

Pesetsky, David (1987) '*Wh-in-situ*: Movement and Unselective Binding', In Eric J. Reuland and Alice G.B. ter Meulen (eds.), *The Representation of (In)definiteness*, pp. 98-129, MIT Press, Cambridge, Mass.

Platzack, Christer (1986) 'The Position of the Finite Verb in Swedish', In Hubert Haider and Martin Prinzhorn (eds.), *Verb Second Phenomena in Germanic Languages*, pp. 27-47, Foris, Dordrecht.

Pollock, Jean-Yves (1989) 'Verb Movement, universal grammar and the Structure of IP', *Linguistic Inquiry* 20, 365-424.

Radford, Andrew (1988) *Transformational Grammar: Cambridge Textbooks in Linguistics*, Cambridge University Press, Cambridge.

Raposo, Eduardo and Juan Uriagereka (1990) 'Long Distance Case Assignment', *Linguistic Inquiry* 21, 505-537.

Rivero, Maria-Luisa (1991) 'Long Head Movement and Negation: Serbo-Croatian vs. Slovak and Czech', *The Linguistic Review* 8, 319-351.

Rizzi, Luigi (1982) *Issues in Italian Syntax*, Foris, Dordrecht.

Rizzi, Luigi (1990a) *Relativized Minimality*, MIT Press, Cambridge, Mass.

Rizzi, Luigi (1990b) 'Speculations on Verb Second', In Joan Mascaro and Marina Nespor (eds), *Grammar in Progress: Glow Essays for Henk van Riemsdijk*, pp.375-386, Foris, Dordrecht.

Rizzi, Luigi (1991) 'Residual Verb Second and the *Wh*-Criterion', *Technical Reports in Formal and Computational Linguistics* 2, Faculty of Letters, University of Geneva, Geneva.

Rizzi, Luigi (1997) 'The Fine Structure of the Left Periphery', In Liliane Haegeman (ed.), *Elements of grammar: Handbook in Generative Syntax*, PP. 281-337, Kluwer, Amsterdam.

Rizzi, Luigi and Ian Roberts (1989) 'Complex Inversion in French', *Probus* 1, 1-30.

Roberts, Ian (1991) 'Excorporation and Minimality', *Linguistic Inquiry* 22, 209-218.

Roberts, Ian (1993) *Verbs and Diachronic Syntax*, Kluwer, Dordrecht.

Roberts, Ian (1997) 'Directionality and Word Order Change in the History of English', In Ans van Kemenade and Nigel Vincent (eds.), *Parameters of Morphosyntactic Change*, pp. 397-426, Cambridge University Press, Cambridge.

Roberts Ian, and Anna Roussou (2003) *Syntactic Change: A Minimalist Approach to Grammaticalization*, Cambridge University Press. Cambridge.

Rochemont, Michael (1986) *Focus in Generative Grammar*, John Benjamins, Amsterdam.

Rooth, Mats (1985) 'Association with Focus', Doctoral Dissertation, University of Massachusetts, Amherst.

Saito, Mamoru (1987) 'An Extension of K.I Harada's *Wh*-Q Binding Analysis', Paper presented at the Fifth annual meeting of the English Linguistic Society of Japan.

Saito, Mamoru (1989) 'Scrambling as Semantically Vacuous A′-Movement', In Mark Baltin and Anthony Kroch (eds.), Alternative Conceptions of Phrase Structure, pp. 182-200, University of Chicago Press, Chicago.

Saito, Mamoru (1992) 'Long Distance Scrambling in Japanese', *The Journal of East Asian Linguistics* 1, 69-118.

Sasaki, Takashi (1996) *Jyodaigo no Koubun to Hyoki*, Hituzi, Tokyo.

Srivastav, Veneeta (1989) 'Hindi *Wh* and Pleonastic Operators', *Proceedings of the Twentieth Annual Meeting of NELS*, pp. 443-457.

Srivastav, Veneeta (1991) 'Subjacency effects at LF: The Case of Hindi *Wh*', *Linguistic Inquiry* 22, 762-769.

Stowell, Tim (1983) 'Subjects across Categories', *The Linguistic Review* 2, 285-312.

Sumangala, Lelwala (1992) 'Long Distance Dependencies: The Syntax of Focus and *WH*-Questions in Sinhala', Doctoral Dissertation, Cornell University, Ithaca.

Takezawa, Koichi (1987) 'A Configurational Approach to Case-Marking in Japanese', Doctoral Dissertation, University of Washington.

Taraldsen, Knut Tarald (1986) 'On Verb Second and the Functional Content of Syntactic Categories', In Hubert Haider and Martin Prinzhorn (eds.), *Verb Second Phenomena in Germanic Languages*, pp. 7-25, Foris, Dordrecht.

Tateishi, Koichi (1994) *The Syntax of Subjects*, Kurosio, Tokyo.

Thiersch, Craig (1978) 'Topics in German Syntax', Doctoral Dissertation, MIT.

Tomaselli, Alessandra (1990) 'Comp as a Licensing Head: An Argument Based on Cliticization', In Joan Mascaró and Marina Nespor (eds.) *Grammar in Progress*, GLOW Essays for Henk van Riemsdijk, pp. 433-445, Foris, Dordrecht.

Travis, Lisa (1984) 'Parameters and Effects of Word Order Variation', Doctoral Dissertation, MIT, Cambridge, Mass.

Tuller, Laurice (1992) 'The Syntax of Postverbal Focus Constructions in Chadic', *Natural Language and Linguistic Theory* 10, 303-334.

Ueyama, Ayumi (1992) 'I-to-C Movement as a Last Resort of Licensing [+WH]', Manuscript, Kyoto University, Kyoto.

Vikner, Sten (1990) 'Verb Movement and the Licensing of NP-Positions in the Germanic Languages', Doctoral Dissertation, University of Stuttgart.

Wahba, Wafaa (1984) '*Wh*-Constructions in Egyptian Arabic', Doctoral Dissertation, University of Illinois, Urbana.

Watanabe, Akira (1992a) '*Wh-in-situ*, Subjacency and Chain Formation', *MIT Occasional Papers in Linguistics* 2, MIT, Cambridge.

Watanabe, Akira (1992b) 'Subjacency and S-structure Movement of *Wh-in-situ*', *Journal of East Asian Linguistics* 1, 255-291.

Watanabe, Akira (2002) 'The Loss of Overt *Wh*-Movement in Old Japanese', In David W. Lightfoot (ed.), *Syntactic Effects of Morphological Change*, pp.179-195, Oxford University Press, Oxford.

Webelhuth, Gert (1989) 'Syntactic Saturation Phenomena and the Modern Germanic Languages', Doctoral Dissertation, University of Massachusetts, Amherst.

Whitman, John (1991) 'String Vacuous V to Comp', Presented at GLOW.

Whitman, John (2000) 'Relabelling', In Susan Pintzuk, George Tsoulas, and Anthony Warner (eds.), *Diachronic Syntax: Models and Mechanisms*, pp. 220-238, Oxford University Press, Oxford.

Whitman, John (2001) 'Kayne 1994: P.143, FN.3', In Alexandrova, Balina M. and Olga Arnudova (eds.) *The Minimalist Parameter*, pp. 77-100, John Benjamins, Amsterdam.

Wilder, Chris and Damir Cavar (1994) 'Long Head Movement?: Verb Movement and Cliticization in Croatian', *Lingua* 93, 1-58.

Yamada, Masahiro (2000) 'Shugo Hyouji *ga* no Seiryoku Kakudai no Yousou', *Kokugo-gaku* 51, 1-14.

Yamada, Masahiro (2001) 'Shugo Hyouji *ga* no Kyouchou Hyougen ni Okeru Seiryoku Kakudai no Yousou', *Kokugo Kokubun* 70-8, 32-48.

Yamada, Takao (1929) *Nihon Bunpooron*, Jitsubunkan, Tokyo.

Yamada, Takao (1938) *Nihon Bunpoo Koogi*, Jitsubunkan, Tokyo.

Yanagida, Seiji (1985) *Muromachi Jidai no Kokugo*, Tokyo Doo, Tokyo.

Yanagida, Yuko (1995) 'Focus Projection and *Wh*-head Movement', Doctoral Dissertation, Cornell University, Ithaca.

Yanagida, Yuko (1996) 'Syntactic QR in *Wh-in-situ* Languages', *Lingua* 99, 21-36.

Yanagida, Yuko (2003a) 'Joudaigo-no Kukouzou to Gojyun-no Seiyaku-nitsuite', *Gengo Bunka Ronshu*, 64, 19-40.

Yanagida, Yuko (2003b) 'Obligatory Movement and Head Parameter: Evidence from Early Classical Japanese', *Sophia Linguistica* 50, 103-116.

Yanagida, Yuko (2003c) 'Focus Movement and the Quantificational Structure of Focus Sensitive Operators', *English Linguistics* 20, 365-389.

Yanagida, Yuko (2004) 'Word Order and Clause Structure in Early Old Japanese', Manuscript, University of Tsukuba.

Zwart, Jan-Wouter (1991) 'Clitics in Dutch: Evidence for the Position of Infl', *Groninger Arbeiten zur Germanistischen Linguistik* 33, 71-92.

Zwart, Jan-Wouter (1993) 'Verb Movement and Complementizer Agreement', *MIT Working Papers in Linguistics* 18, 297-340.

Zwart, Jan-Wouter (1997) 'The Germanic SOV Languages and the Universal Base Hypothesis', In Liliane Haegeman (ed.), *The New Comparative Syntax*, pp. 246-267, Longman, London.

INDEX

[A]
adverbial focus particles — 103
adverbs of quantification — 145, 147
Amakusa Heike — 95, 104

[B]
Baker — 3

[C]
categorial change — 91
categorial reanalysis — 89
Chadic languages — 18
Chomsky — 3, 26, 136
clitic pronouns — 121
copula — 80

[D]
definiteness effect — 160
Diesing — 35, 135, 153, 162
Discourse Representation Theory — 148

[E]
ECP — 53
EPP-feature — 127
excorporation — 61
exhaustive listing — 14, 135
Extraction Constraint — 37

[F]
feature strength — 3, 50
focal mapping — 142
focus Criterion — 21
focus particles — 79
focus prominent language — 105
focus-background — 139
Fukui — 129
functional category — 126

[G]
Gelderen — 92
generalized pied-piping — 128

[H]
head internal relative clauses — 112
Head Movement Constraint — 51
head parameter — 126
Heim — 35, 151, 152
Herburger — 140
Hoji — 43
Horvath — 15, 71

[K]
Kadmon — 150
Kageyama — 91
Kakari-musubi — 6, 113
Kakari-particles — 103
Kato — 116
Kayne — 88, 123, 124
Kemenade — 90
Kim — 11, 42
Kishimoto — 7
Kiss — 1
Koji — 100, 110
Konkoumyou Saishou Oukyou — 105, 116
Kuno — 134
Kuroda — 112
Kuwabara — 133

[L]
Laka — 84, 116
Lasnik and Saito — 38, 72
last resort condition — 60
last resort principle — 61
Lehmann — 105
Lewis — 145
lexical category — 126
Lightfoot — 124
Linear Correspondence Axiom — 88, 124
Los — 91

[M]
Manyogana — 108
Manyoshu — 98, 105, 106
Mapping Hypothesis — 35, 154
McDaniel — 9

183

Milsark 160
minimal domain 89
Minimal Link Condition 26, 160
Miyagawa 106
Motohashi 94, 115

[N]
neutral description 14, 135
Nishigauchi 26
Nomura 101, 119

[O]
Object Shift 115
Ohno 104

[P]
Parsons 141
Pesetsky 45
Phase Impenetrability Condition 156
Pollock 62
presupposition 143
Presuppositional NP constraint 164
Projection Principle 127

[Q]
Q-particle 41

[R]
reanalysis 87
relabeling 89
Rizzi 52, 60, 84, 103
Roberts 60, 84, 88, 124
Roussou 88

[S]
small clause 98

Srivastav 10
Stranded Affix Filter 62, 132
Subjacency 38, 155
subject prominent language 1, 105
Sumangala 7

[T]
Takezawa 97
Tale of Heike 104
Tateishi 22
that-trace effects 72
topic prominent language 1
Topicalization 119
Travis 51
Tuller 18

[U]
uniqueness implication 152
unselective quantifiers 148

[V]
Verb Second 56

[W]
Wahba 9
Watanabe 26, 102
Wh-Criterion 52, 68
Whitman 89
Wh-Parameter 133
Wilder and Cavar 63, 131

[Y]
Yamada 95, 96

[Z]
Zwart 57, 59, 124

【著者紹介】
柳田優子（やなぎだゆうこ）
慶應義塾大学文学部（史学科）卒業。オレゴン大学修士課程（言語学）をへて、1995年コーネル大学にて博士号（言語学）取得。1992年　高知大学教育学部講師、1994年　高知大学教育学部助教授、2001年　筑波大学現代語・現代文化学系助教授、現在、筑波大学人文社会科学研究科助教授。

The Syntax of FOCUS and WH-Questions in Japanese
A Cross-Linguistic Perspective

発行	2005年2月25日　初版1刷
定価	11000円＋税
著者	©柳田優子
発行者	松本　功
印刷所	三美印刷株式会社
製本所	田中製本印刷株式会社
発行所	有限会社ひつじ書房

〒112-0002 東京都文京区小石川5-21-5
Tel. 03-5684-6871 Fax. 03-5684-6872
郵便振替00120-8-142852
toiawase@hituzi.co.jp
http://www.hituzi.co.jp

造本には充分注意しておりますが、落丁・乱丁などがございましたら、小社かお買上げ書店にておとりかえいたします。
ご意見、ご感想など、小社までにお寄せ下されば幸いです。

ISBN4-89476-239-0 C3081

ひつじ研究叢書（言語編）

36. 現代日本語の疑問表現―疑いと確認要求
    宮崎和人著　5460円
37. 事態概念の記号化に関する認知言語学的研究
    谷口一美著　6510円
38. 日本語態度動詞文の情報構造
    小野正樹著　9870円
39. 日本語述語の統語構造と語形成
    ―意味役割の表示と状態述語、心理述語、使役構文からの提言
    外崎淑子著　8820円

★表示の値段は税込価格です。
★月刊『言語』には毎月、広告をだしておりますので、ご覧ください。
★最新の情報はひつじ書房のホームページに掲載しています。
    http://www.hituzi.co.jp/をご覧ください。

シリーズ 言語学と言語教育

4. 言語教育の新展開―牧野成一教授古希記念論文集
   鎌田修・筒井通雄・畑佐由紀子・ナズキアン富美子・岡まゆみ著　8400円
5. 第二言語習得とアイデンティティ
   窪田光男著　7350円

★表示の値段は税込価格です。
★月刊『言語』には毎月、広告をだしておりますので、ご覧ください。
★最新の情報はひつじ書房のホームページに掲載しています。
　http://www.hituzi.co.jp/をご覧ください。

シリーズ 文と発話

1. 「伝達道具」としての文と発話
   　　串田秀也・定延利之・伝康晴編　予価3360円
2. 「単位」としての文と発話
   　　串田秀也・定延利之・伝康晴編　予価3360円
3. 時間の中の文と発話
   　　串田秀也・定延利之・伝康晴編　予価3360円

★2005年夏から順次刊行予定。
★表示の値段は税込価格です。
★月刊『言語』には毎月、広告をだしておりますので、ご覧ください。
★最新の情報はひつじ書房のホームページに掲載しています。
　http://www.hituzi.co.jp/をご覧ください。